*Working with Children in Hospitals*

*Working*

# EMMA N. PLANK
## WITH THE ASSISTANCE OF MARLENE A. RICHIE

# *with Children in Hospitals*
## A GUIDE FOR THE PROFESSIONAL TEAM

*Reprinted Third Edition*

To the memory of
Lili E. Peller
and
Annie Reich, M.D.

# *Tribute*

The third edition of this book was supported through the generosity of Dr. and Mrs. Robert M. Eiben. Dr. Eiben, Emeritus Professor of Pediatric Neurology at MetroHealth Medical Center, was a faculty member in 1955 when Emma Plank joined the staff. He became a major advocate of her work and the child life profession. Dr. Fredrick C. Robbins, Professor and Director of the Department of Pediatrics and Contagious Disease at MetroHealth Medical Center, hired Emma Plank to address the needs of hospitalized children. Emma N. Plank is recognized for her teachings which impacted the psychosocial management of children in the hospitals and health care settings.

## Emma N. Plank
## 1905 – 1990

| | |
|---|---|
| 1951 – 1952 | Senior Instructor in Child Development<br>Western Reserve University, Cleveland, Ohio<br>(Presently Case Western Reserve University), Cleveland, Ohio |
| 1952 – 1964 | Assistant Professor in Child Development<br>Western Reserve University, Cleveland, Ohio<br>(Presently Case Western Reserve University), Cleveland, Ohio |
| 1950 – 1953 | Director, Children's House<br>(Presently Hanna Perkins Center for Child Development), Cleveland, Ohio |
| 1953 – 1955 | Assistant Professor of Education<br>Western Reserve University,<br>(Presently Case Western Reserve University), Cleveland, Ohio |
| 1955 – 1972 | Founder and Director of The Child Life and Education Program City Hospital<br>(Presently The Children's Hospital At MetroHealth Medical Center), Cleveland, Ohio |
| 1964 – 1972 | Associate Professor in Child Development<br>Western Reserve University,<br>(Presently Case Western Reserve University), Cleveland, Ohio |
| 1972 | Professor Emeritus of Child Development<br>Case Western Reserve University, Cleveland, Ohio |

# Preface to the Third Edition

As The Children's Hospital at MetroHealth Medical Center celebrates the 50th anniversary of the founding of the first university affiliated Child Life and Education Program, in Cleveland, Ohio, it is fitting to reflect upon Emma N. Plank's contributions to the well being of pediatric patients and families and for making Child Life the recognized profession it is today.

Emma N. Plank's book, *Working with Children in Hospitals,* was the first text to describe and document the stressful impact of hospitalization on children and define the "Child Life Worker" as an essential and unique professional member of the health care team.

This pertinent book, now in the third edition, can only emphasis the magnitude of Emma N. Plank's work as a pioneer and teacher whose longstanding concepts have stood the test of time. As she stated in the second edition, "I sincerely hope that this book will again reach those who try so hard to make children's hospitalizations a stimulation rather than a deterrent to child development." We are pleased to be making this meaningful book available again to students and professionals alike.

- The Child Life and Education Staff
The Children's Hospital, at MetroHealth Medical Center
Cleveland, Ohio  2005

# Foreword

The care of children in hospitals has changed remarkably in recent years. Scientific advances have modified the kinds of treatment available and to some extent altered the spectrum of diseases to be seen in the hospital. For instance, a larger proportion of patients admitted are undergoing surgical procedures and all are subjected to more extensive investigation and treatment than was true in the past. Doctors are more specialized and often the physicians caring for a child in the hospital are not involved with his long-term overall care. Then too, with the shortage of nurses and the increased demands on their time they are less able to concern themselves with emotional needs of the patients. Thus, it is possible for the hospital situation to become excessively impersonal with a great deal of attention being paid to the child's illness and too little to his feelings. Indeed, as a perceptive colleague of mine has often said, "Someone must defend the child against the system." Unfortunately, there is all too much truth in this statement. It is as the child's advocate against the system that the child-care worker fulfills her most important role.

In all fairness, most hospitals have had programs designed to occupy and amuse children and, in some instances, these have been quite elaborate. The "play lady" is a well established institution. However, the concept expressed by Mrs. Plank and her associates that there is need for special training and skills unique to the child-care worker is not so generally realized. The well intentioned volunteer who likes children still has her place, but it would seem that the needs are greater than she can fulfill. It is our contention that child care in the hospital should be under the direction of persons who have had experience and training in child development (both psychologic and physical), education and diversional techniques. They must also have sufficient understanding of medical matters and the administrative structure within the hospital so that they can function comfortably in the hospital environment. It is with the development of such persons in mind that this book has been prepared. It has been kept in mind, however, that smaller units cannot support specially trained personnel. The many practical suggestions will be helpful to nurses and others in such situations.

The authors have had a wealth of experience in the actual development of a program of child care on a pediatric service in a general hospital supported by public funds. Their program started as an experiment, but has become an integral part of the pediatric department. Unexpected dividends have accrued. Not only has it improved the actual care of the hospitalized child, but it has made major contributions in the teaching of medical students, nurses, and pediatric house officers. The value of the child-care program to the function of the department as a whole would be difficult to overestimate.

The success of such a program is dependent upon the caliber of people conducting it and there are presently few who are adequately prepared. However, with recognition of the need it is to be hoped that more competent well-motivated individuals will be encouraged to seek out the requisite training.

F. C. Robbins, M.D.
*Dean, School of Medicine*
*Professor of Pediatrics*
*Case Western Reserve University*

# *Preface to the Second Edition*

The second edition of *Working with Children in Hospitals* contains some new materials, particularly in the area of children's spontaneous writing and drawing (see Chapter 8) and in new ways to prepare for procedures (see Chapter 3). Some epidemiologic changes like the decrease of tuberculosis and the disappearance of poliomyelitis motivated the rewriting of Chapter 9. Photographs have been added which we hope speak directly of children's needs and strengths.

Since the first edition of this book came out, child-care workers in departments of pediatrics throughout the United States and Canada have formed a new organization, The American Association for Child Care in Hospitals, open to all professionals working with children in medical settings. This organization has liaison members from the Child Development Section of the American Academy of Pediatrics, from the Academy of Child Psychiatry, and from the Society of Pediatric Psychology, the organizations that formulated so well the needs on which we build.

I sincerely hope that this book will again reach those who try so hard to make children's hospitalizations a stimulation rather than a deterrent to child development.

E.N.P.

# *Acknowledgements*

First of all I want to thank the Cleveland Foundation whose grant allowed us to start the Child Life and Education Program at Cleveland Metropolitan General Hospital as a two-year demonstration project before it became integrated into the hospital's budget. The Foundation assisted again in the preparation of this book by granting funds for an artist on the staff, for photography and its reproduction, and for an honorarium for a former worker who helped in the preparation of the manuscript.

This book is possible because many people brought their skills to develop the program which I will describe. Some of the observations of children were written by Dale Havre, M.D., some photographs were taken by Patricia A. Caughey, M.D. Both carried out this work in partial fulfillment of the requirements of the Project Teaching Program of the Medical Curriculum, Western Reserve University, School of Medicine. Mr. Herman Lorenzo of the Photography Division of our hospital contributed some photographs.

Carla Horwood, M.D., Wilma Rice, M.A., Marlene A. Ritchie, M.N., and Elizabeth Diaz, M.A., were the child-care workers who worked out many of the practical details of our plan and contributed pertinent observations and some photographs. Kirstie B. Rossen did the drawings.

My special thanks go to my friends Ruth Dross, Helen Hallfors and the late Lili Peller, social group worker, nursing educator and child analyst, who read the manuscript and helped me with their detailed constructive critique.

The reproduction of a section from Sean O'Casey's *I Knock at the Door* is by the gracious permission of the Macmillan Company, and Macmillan and Company, Ltd., copyright owners.

# Contents

1. A Child Enters the Hospital 1
2. Interaction, Empathy, and Withdrawal in Children 9
3. Preparation for Surgery 14
4. Working Through Feelings After Surgery 25
5. If Death Occurs on a Children's Ward 32
6. Play and Activities 38
7. Learning in the Hospital 48
8. Children Tell Stories and Draw 58
9. A Child Life and Education Program 70

Appendixes
    A. Crafts and Experiments 80
    B. Equipment and Supplies 83
    C. Information for Parents 85
    D. "A Letter to Blackie" 92
    E. Physiological Drawings 99

Bibliography 103

# 1/A Child Enters the Hospital

When an adult is hospitalized, his normal way of living and activity is interrupted. He can resume the cycle when his health is restored. Children can not do this. The growing child can not afford to interrupt the cycle of his living and growth.

When a child is hospitalized, the hospital has to take on tasks beyond its healing function, tasks which must be accomplished so the rhythm of life and growth can go on. The child's normal way of living involves relating to other children, to grownups, and to play and learning. It has to be skillfully fitted into a day filled with diagnostic and treatment procedures. The task is complicated by the threat of the illness itself, of operations, and the possible nearness of death. These are the matters with which this book deals.

How to work out a good living pattern for children in a hospital will depend on its size and resources. In the small hospital with only a few beds for children, all activities and planning will center around the nurse. Children's hospitals may have it easier than others because administration will, by the very nature of the institution, be focused on children and their needs. The larger general hospital needs perhaps the most careful planning for its services to children. The experiences which prompted this book come from such a hospital.

We in the Department of Pediatrics at Cleveland Metropolitan General Hospital feel that the insights we gained and the practices we evolved may be of help to professional workers in settings of very different kinds than ours, because the basic problems are the same: grief at separation from home, anxiety about mutilation of one's body at surgery, submission to immobility, and the many other adjustments that the child has to make to illness and to the hospital regime. We hope that the variety of problems and our attempts to solve them will allow others to find suggestions for their own situation.

We have learned to substitute knowledge and comprehension for fear of the unknown and the misunderstood. To apply this to a child's hospitalization brings an array of questions. We have asked ourselves how we can best serve the child who is about to enter the hospital; what we can do for him when he is there; and how to help him to return to normal living.

Our task starts right at admission. We all agree that a child should not be tricked into coming to the hospital but should know as much about it as possible, and that the mother is the key person in preparing him. Nevertheless, parent and child need our patient and unstinting help at admission.

When the child arrives, the hospital staff has to be aware of the give and take between child and parent. A quick assessment of the parents' strength or of their inability to help their children can make admission very much easier for the child. The hospital staff will especially need to review with the mother what the child has been told, whether he knows that he will have to stay, and that he has been reassured that mother will be around as much as possible and come back soon to visit him.

Ideally a child will be well prepared by his family and will know why he is in the hospital. But what about emergency admissions, a child that does not live with his family, or a mother who can not help her child on account of her own excessive fears or who for some other reason won't cooperate? What about children from a foreign language background or the very young ones who do not yet communicate by language understandable to us?

The mother's presence throughout all steps of the admission procedures is important for all children, but particularly for those who can not yet communicate with others. In that age group, the greatest threat is the fear of being abandoned by the mother in such a weird place.

Many young children find almost everything in the hospital unfamiliar: from the elevator to the hospital gown, from urinal and bed pan to having their meals served on a tray. Also, people look and sound very different from those at home. Most children will have had experience with hypodermic needles, but not with x-rays, blood work, or electrocardiograms.

Therefore, some hospitals in this country and in England have made arrangements that mothers may live in with their very young children. This

*In isolation . . . .*

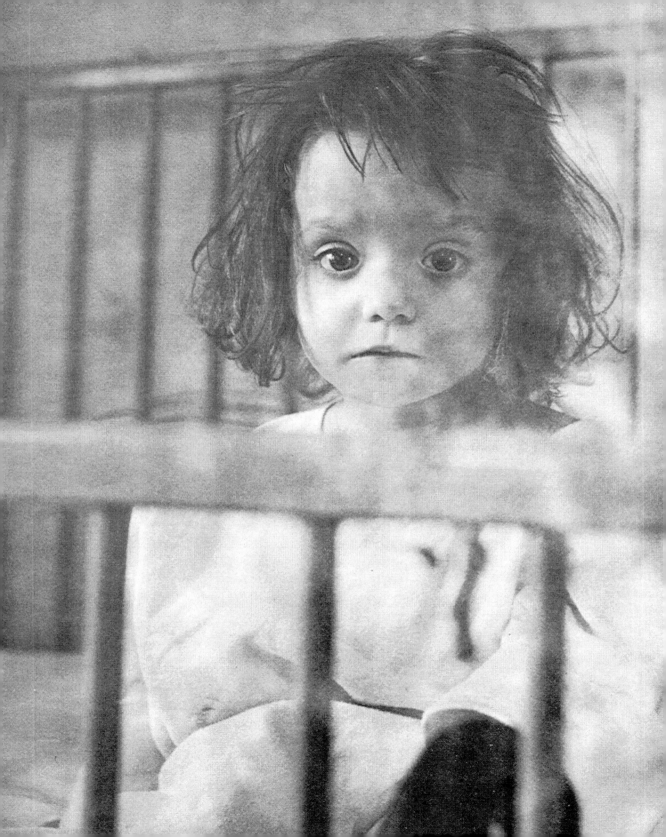

plan is based on the same thinking as the rooming-in at birth. It will not fit all family situations but may be of real value for some. In countries like India and Japan mothers move into the hospital with their children as a matter of routine. They take care of them and cook their meals. These countries recognize shortcomings in their system and are trying to change it in our direction, while we hope to move away from too much professional efficiency around a sick child and to have mothers closer.

What advice can we offer a mother on preparing her young child? She can walk or drive by the hospital ahead of time and tell her child that he will go there—for instance, to have an operation so he won't have such bad colds any more. Some mothers don't like to talk about this, because they have disagreeable memories of their own hospitalizations. But it is good to tell the child that he will be in a room with two, four, or ten other children, or whatever the situation may be. Mother should also tell him how eating and sleeping will differ from what he is used to at home, that there will be a playroom to play in; but she should be sure to say why he is going to the hospital. To children it may easily look like punishment.

A mother often finds this preparation hard, and she makes up a glowing picture of how nice things are going to be: e.g., she will stress that Johnnie will have ice cream after his tonsils are out, without mentioning that his throat will hurt upon waking up from the anesthesia and that he won't like to talk much either. However, she can reassure him that he will feel much better the next morning.

The mother herself needs to be reassured that it's only natural for a young child to cry when she has to leave. She should not avoid this by sneaking out. The crying is hard on parents and child, but the child's disappointment after the mother's sneaking out is far worse. She should also tell him when she will be back and when his daddy will come to see him. She can assure him that she will know how to find him if he is not in his bed, but busy in the playroom or wherever he is. Some children cling to the place where their mother left them and are petrified if they have to move from their bed, since the hospital is such an unfamiliar place.

The older child will understand that his mother won't abandon him in the hospital. But he will worry about having to give up his independence. It seems to these children that wilful adults—doctors and nurses—can do whatever they please to their bodies: draw blood, enforce medication, control their body functions. The greatest fear is to be "put to sleep" before an operation.

Although doctors and nurses will give the child detailed information needed to prepare him for his specific surgery, the mother has a function in this, too. She should repeat the facts and reassure the child that she trusts his doctor.

Each hospital will want its own information folder for parents. The text of the booklet we use, which may lend itself to adaptation for other hospitals, will be found in Appendix C.

We don't need to stress the desirability of closeness between parents and child during the period of hospitalization. It is most encouraging to see how visiting hours have been liberalized and how the medical and nursing staffs are aware of child-parent interaction and take extra time for talking to help a child settle down if he is upset after a parent's visit, rather than to curb visiting.

With youngsters on the threshold of adolescence, the doctor will want to take an active part in the preparation, often even in talking to the child alone to get his cooperation for hospitalization. These young people need special consideration and should be given the much needed status and privacy, and as much independence as possible. They should have a living unit of their own, neither with adults nor with young children. Some may want to be around younger children part of the day, but in the daily routines like body care, food, and sleep, their age should be recognized.

The hospital staff has to be especially alert in helping children to "settle in" who don't have the support of a functioning family.

The youngster from a children's home or from the detention home of the Juvenile Court will need particular attention. To these children especially, their illness often seems like retribution, and this makes it more difficult to treat them. They may react with depression or real belligerence.

Children also become sick at times when their mothers are not able to be with them—perhaps through the mother's confinement in a maternity ward. Every effort should be made to let the child know what happened to mother and to try to establish contact between them.

Language barriers can be formidable obstacles. We can readily identify with what Gulliver went through in Brobdingnag. There is often a need to find an adult with knowledge of the specific language to help both the child and his family to understand what is going on and being planned. However, children can be the best interpreters for each other: it is amazing how they understand when adults don't. Watch out, they may also understand what we say when we don't expect it.

One anecdote may illustrate how children listen intently to things said in their presence and how erroneous it would be to assume that scientific terms, because they are outside their range of vocabulary, can not arouse a child's anxiety. Ronnie, an eight-year-old, suffered from a kidney ailment. One day on rounds, the physicians discussed the edema in his abdomen. A little later, Ronnie came to the playroom quite upset and said, "The doctors said I still cannot go home, I have a demon in my tummy." He knew what a demon was—he had often been called that when he angered his grandmother.

At emergency admissions, the antennae of the worker must be out in all directions to be ready to help these children and their families.

There is a special group of accidents that can occur when the relationship between a child and his parents is under strain. The child may have been injured because he did not obey, or because nobody cared enough to watch him. He may never have learned to establish controls from within. The guilt feelings then on the child's or the parents' side can be very strong and may have to be dealt with. Accidental poisoning, burns, injuries with household implements, accidents on the street can fall into this category.

The workers' first task here is to help the child to settle down and to learn to relate and to trust them. They have to guard against a repetition of the relationship which may have led to the mishap. These children are often over-aggressive, constantly in movement, and "into everything". They do not take easily to discipline in a group and are not dependable to set their own controls. A deep disappointment in their parents may be the reason that they are not ready to trust anybody. They have to feel our sympathy as well as our ability to set controls.

Elective admissions for serious procedures are normally planned and discussed long beforehand in the doctor's office or in the out-patient clinic. The doctor and the nurse can be very helpful in preparing mothers and children for them. The steps we took before five-year-old Harold entered the hospital for corrective heart surgery may be a good example. This type of operation is anticipated long ahead of time, and therefore the fears of the family and the child are of long standing. These fears may be expressed openly or may be bravely covered up, but they will be present in any case and need to be worked with.

A nursing student had been assigned to start the preparation during Harold's clinic visits several weeks prior to admission. She talked to his mother first to find out how much the boy knew of the planned operation.

She learned that he had been told about it in a fairly accurate, reassuring way. The mother was encouraged to tell him more and received detailed information from the nursing student what to point out to Harold. During his last visit to the clinic several days prior to admission for surgery, the nurse took Harold and his mother to the ward to which he would be admitted. He saw convalescent, but also bed-bound children, the dining area and the playroom, and met the charge nurse and the child-care worker. Both he and his mother looked rather solemn and left after a short visit. But now they had something concrete to talk about and they were more at ease when Harold was admitted.

This was essentially preparation for hospital admission and would not have been much different if no operation had been involved. It was pretty much like preparation for nursery school or kindergarten, where we are also likely to let the mother bring the child in for a short visit before he is entered.

What is the "child-care worker" we have just mentioned? What does she do? Throughout this book we will talk about "child-care workers." We have called them that in lieu of a better descriptive term. Neither "teacher" nor "play lady" nor "play therapist," which are used in other hospitals, seem to fit the function.

The child-care worker is a person on the clinical team who is responsible for the children at play and at meal times, or in the hospital school, but is not involved in nursing function as such, though she may help prepare children for medical procedures or surgery through such activities as dramatic play or earnest and factual conversation in the playroom.

Ideally, the nurse is able to assume many of the child-care worker's functions, and she often does. Many of the suggestions we will make in describing a child-centered program can be and have been used by nurses who have served children in this way along with their many other responsibilities. The shortage of nurses, though, and the unpredictable emergencies that are part of the nurse's day make it unrealistic to rely on her alone in a larger pediatric department. There she finds the child-care worker her ally.

*Johnny had to come to the playroom in bed. Too weak to be active himself, he is cheered up by his friends and their puppets.*

# 2/Interaction, Empathy, and Withdrawal in Children

As we were looking for better ways of helping children to adjust to the hospital experience, we found strong assistance in the spontaneous interaction among the children themselves. In this chapter we will talk about this interaction, but also about withdrawn children who lack spontaneity and need the help of the adults to adjust. In a later chapter we will describe planned interaction when we discuss programming for children in play and in school work.

We can do a great deal for spontaneous interaction by the grouping of the children's beds and organization of their activities. Here we have to move away from thinking about grouping that applies to healthy children. The common denominator in the hospital is not primarily age or sex, nor the socio-cultural background: it is the anxious uncertainty through separation and pain which creates a strong bond. The support children give each other works in both directions: older children can function as protectors or playmates for younger ones, while the helplessness of the very young, and the delight in seeing developmental changes in an infant or toddler, can act as a morale-builder for children slightly older and up to adolescence. We feel strongly that the age range on a ward should be wider than customary since children profit from at least part-time contact with others of different age levels.

A remarkable amount of helpful interaction goes on without our planning, but it needs our quick recognition to allow its development. It also needs to be stopped decisively if it should turn into a burden for a child. I would like to illustrate by using examples from different services of our hospital. In our first illustration, from our contagious disease division, the spontaneous interaction showed itself in an almost uncanny empathy of an older youngster with a little boy.

Howard, age ten, and Frank, four and one-half years old, were both hospitalized for tuberculous meningitis. They shared an isolation room for about two months. Frank's parents, who were separated and lived about forty miles from the hospital, could visit him only rarely. He was much sicker than Howard. He had been comatose for about four weeks and was still semicomatose when Howard was admitted and this observation began. It was extremely difficult for the nursing personnel to care for Frank in the semicomatose stage. Any attempt to touch him for comfort, treatment, or nursing purposes brought piercing screams. Howard, separated by a glass partition, had not been unconscious but was completely inactive. He had just begun to look at television programs for short periods as his only activity.

My contact with these children was a very fleeting one. I would stop at their room once or twice a day, trying to find signs of responsiveness to see when they would profit from more stimulation. During one of those visits Frank screamed again when his linen had to be changed. Howard called to the nurse, "If you cover him up he'll stop screaming," and true enough Frank stopped. When I visited the next time and asked Howard how they were, he said, "If I tell Frank to look at TV he'll look," and the little boy who otherwise was completely rigid did turn his eyes to look.

From then on we decided to let Howard be the one to tell us when Frank was ready for a new step. He would know at which angle the child could drink through a straw (he had had to be fed by tube for a long time before), which juices he preferred, and finally proceeded to help Frank say a word or two. The medical staff was deeply touched by Howard's unfailing intuition about Frank's needs. He would demonstrate to Frank how to stretch his legs for his exercises in physical therapy, which the skillful therapist had not been able to do, and Frank, as if in a trance, followed the example. When Frank cried, the only thing that could comfort him was Howard's voice.

When Howard was ready to be transferred to the convalescent unit, we decided to move Frank along even though he was completely immobile and had only partially recovered his vision. We feared a setback if he lost his only friend and protector at this point. At the same time we made it clear to Howard that he could get up now and join other children at play. But the two boys still shared their room for sleeping and Howard would stop by to share an occasional meal or play a little with Frank. When Frank just started to sit up, discharge time for Howard approached. One day when I fed Frank and needed an implement I asked Howard to get it for us. "Get it yourself," was the answer, a very appropriate one for a ten-year-old who now could let his defense down and did not have to help the other child constantly in order to keep his own anxiety in check.

Both children did well after Howard's discharge. When Frank left two months later he had formed strong relationships with the nurses and child-care worker and had learned to talk and play again.

The strong bond between these children did not stem from saintly altruism. It was produced by Howard's anxiety, but nevertheless was most helpful to both children in their very difficult time in the isolation room. The child-care staff had to decide on the right moment to relieve Howard of his self-sought function and let an adult form the bridge between Frank and the outside world. (One of the touching elements of this case was the fact that ten-year-old Howard was black, and little Frank a Eurasian.)

We could observe another example of empathy in two little girls hospitalized at a month's interval for burns.

Ida, age eight, who was almost ready for discharge, spent some time every day, masked and gowned, to play with three-year-old Jean whose lesions were still open. Jean had to be protected from infection and only people who used isolation techniques could be with her. Ida was patient and loving with Jean—while she could be quite angry and demanding with others.

Six-year-old Jack, confined by traction to his bed with Perthes Disease (a growth difficulty in the hip) was an "angry young man." His prolonged immobility was very hard for him. He asked that Susie, a two-year-old with delayed motor development, who could not walk yet, be put on his bed for play. With infinite patience he showed her how to use some manipulative toys. The delight was mutual when Susie succeeded in using them.

Susie also helped a sulking thirteen-year-old diabetic girl to regain some interest outside herself. The little girl's firm attempts at walking brought out the eagerness of the thirteen-year-old to give her the little assistance she needed to take her first steps.

There are on the other hand withdrawn children who do not easily enter into a friendly give-and-take with others. They demand the special attention of one adult. In the hospital, there is no time to lose to help a withdrawn child out of his shell. He may be frozen into inactivity through grief or fear. We have to find some clues to be able to help or reassure him. Allowing such a child to stay close to the adult is one way. We can try to involve him in some kind of solitary play, because others often frighten him.

These children usually prefer quiet activities which require more observation than creativity. They look for a a quiet corner of the room to be in. Often they like to watch pets. One three-year-old who had been quite apathetic, laughed out loud when he saw a rabbit take a huge bite of carrot, but he stayed a safe distance away.

Solitary play with water, sawdust, or play dough may bring a response, but interest is stifled for many children if they fear punishment for getting wet or making a mess, so it is a good thing to give the child an apron and to tell him that if some spills it is easy to clean up—and to show how easy it is. The little mess you make and clean up often strikes a funny point and the child laughs.

Soap bubbles may be a first step to sociability as the child watches a bubble he has made bounce out into the room and vanish as it touches an object. These children usually sit as observers at the edge of a group activity. If children can be taken outdoors to play, many a withdrawn child comes alive at the swing and the slide and often makes friends more rapidly in this more natural setting.

It is helpful if an adult can hold a young child on his lap or can walk around the playroom with such an anxious child, letting him set the pace and showing him things which catch his eye. When something holds his interest, take it out for him to play with. When it is time for the child to leave the playroom, it helps maintain the friendly relationship if he can take something to his bedside—a stuffed animal, a plant to care for, or a small vehicle or doll. The playroom can have a shelf from which children may choose things to take with them.

The withdrawn older child often responds to a challenge—for example, "How well can you play checkers? Do you think you can beat me?" They respond to crafts which require little creativity but produce goodlooking results. Such projects should require very simple directions, or none at all. Examples: making and painting plaster-of-Paris figures; gluing together model planes, cars, or boats.

Youngsters respond to being given tasks in which they can unaggressively be a leader—like running the film strip projector, or calling the numbers or cards for bingo or lotto. They feel that they matter if they can repair something for the playroom worker (choose something which you know the child can do well and which isn't too time consuming). The child-care worker has to show her sincere interest in a child through her warmth, but also through giving the child responsibility.

The withdrawn older child will be in the back row in watching a movie. A girl may enjoy having a little one on her lap. She can respond to some one who has greater need for comfort than she.

Even the withdrawn child can be helped through spontaneous interaction. We can see it in a wide range of activities. Older children may want to be with younger ones and play with them or help watch them. If they have lost some confidence in their own worth, helping a younger child may restore just that. Toddlers gain by having older children around them, whose competition for the attention of the adults is on a different emotional level. It is soothing to be spoken to or rocked or played with on a mat on the floor.

Shyness or a great dependence on the mother may have been personality characteristics of a child before hospitalization. They become more accentuated through experiences of pain and fear.

Other children may find it hard to relate because they come from a socio-economic background vastly different from the hospital culture. Food and sleeping arrangements and play, life's main comforters, may be so different in their home that they bring withdrawal instead of pleasure and relaxation. If we suspect such reasons for a child's sadness we certainly can try to modify some practices, including our expectations in the use of play materials.

# 3/Preparation for Surgery

One may question whether anybody but the surgeon and the anesthetist should have part in preparing a child for surgery. They certainly are the ones who initiate the preparation and give the child the reason for an operation and how it will help him to get well.

The doctors give as many details as they think are warranted in a given case. But, as in other phases of a child's growth, it is not enough to be told a fact once or twice; it has to be assimilated. To truly understand something unknown and fearful, a child needs opportunities to come back to it in his own time. Nurses, playroom workers, and physical therapists therefore often see more of the apprehension and anxiety preceding an operation than the doctor does. They have to do something about it. The best way is to plan jointly. The nurse usually lets the child-care worker know if she feels that a child needs more than the routine preparation she has already given.

As with other things of real importance for children, questions may come in a disguised form and at unexpected, certainly at unscheduled, times. Because the play room is so remote from medical procedures, the children have often found it a safe place to show these fears and to open up for further talks and explanations.

The help that we can give the child patient in preparing him for surgery will always be meaningful, but we have of course to gear it to the child. His age, his personality, his previous medical experience, and the nature of the impending procedure all make a difference. In our experience, children who have had a troubled relationship to their mothers since early childhood or who grew up without fathers are particularly vulnerable.

Fear is not necessarily diminished if a child has already previously experienced surgery or anesthesia. Panic can be evident even before minor procedures. The memory of the smell of ether particularly is recalled with anxiety and unease. The preparations for operations which involve danger, permanent damage, or long convalescence are most delicate but also offer the highest rewards. Our examples will therefore be largely drawn from this area, though, of course, the great majority of operations, such as tonsillectomies, intrude much less violently into the child's life.

Observations of play quite often give us the clue as to how to prepare a child more thoroughly for an impending procedure. We want the child's conscious participation in this process. First he has to know and to trust us and to believe in our honesty, then we have to be able to help relieve some anxieties heightened by his fantasies. Not all we tell him is future unpleasantness: we can also reassure him that sedatives and anesthesia are worth their discomfort because they will keep him from feeling any of the pain of the operation itself. But essentially preparation is learning about things that seem dangerous, and learning them in the way children learn—through the senses, visual, auditory, tactile, olfactory; and through handling of the feelings involved.

Actual equipment, such as anesthesia masks that children can manipulate or put on their faces, caps, gowns, and masks that they can try on, will help in the preparation. Of course, we will not include any details of the surgery itself, as the child will not be awake while these happen, but we will tell him what he will find when he awakes.

Let us see how a four-year-old responded (as recorded by his child-care worker):

*Gary had been given routine preparation for an operation (lung biopsy) by his doctor and his nurse. He became more anxious and aggressive than before, but did not talk about the operation itself until the morning it was scheduled to take place.*

*Gary came into the play room and said, "I'm going to have my operation today, Play-lady, but, not until my mama comes."*

*"Oh, is it today? Well, did the doctors tell you where the operation was going to be?"*

*"No," he hesitated, "the nurse told me."*

*"What did she tell you about the operation?"*

*"It's going to make me well."*

*"Did she tell you what would happen when you go for the operation?"*

*He did not seem to know and said he didn't know where the operation would be, but he knew that being operated meant getting cut.*

*We looked at a picture book designed to help prepare children for surgery. I mentioned that the little boy in the book was sick and that the doctor said he needed an operation, whereupon Gary shouted "I'm not sick! How will it get shut if they cut it?"*

*I explained how the wound is sewed and bandaged. Again he pointed out the area to be operated and then asked how long the bandage would be there. When the picture of the anesthetic mask appeared, he said, "What's that?"*

*I asked if he had seen one before, and he said no, but pointed to the holes and said "Air goes in here." I brought a mask to show him what it was like. I told him how the doctor might ask him to count, and he volunteered that he could count to three.*

*As this was to be a lung operation, I knew that Gary would wake up in an oxygen tent. So I told him that people sometimes sleep in a little plastic tent after their operation. He said he wouldn't like that at all.*

*When his mother came he ran to her and said he was going to have an operation. He complained that he was hungry and wanted her to buy ice cream. He spent most of the rest of the time walking around with his mother and sailing boats in a pan of water.*

*When the surgery cart came, he began to cry and asked if he had to go. "I don't want to go. Will I have to have that thing in my mouth—that thing in the book?"*

*"Do you mean the balloon you'll blow up? It doesn't go into your mouth, but you need it to make you sleepy."*

*Mother was with him. He didn't cry loudly but whined that he didn't want to go. He was given his "shot" and then seemed to have a hard time choosing who would lift him on the cart. The mother did not seem to want to, so I did. Gary said he was afraid he would get another shot and again cried that he didn't want to go and didn't want the mask.*

*While waiting for the elevator, the mother told him she had an operation when she was little and that everything would be all right. She asked him not to cry and told him what they would play with when the operation was over. When he was wheeled into the elevator he had stopped crying. His mother went to the operating floor with him and then returned.*

*The discomfort caused by his thoracotomy tube made it hard for Gary to talk the next day, but he managed. He was especially interested in knowing whether his mother remembered the things she had told him just before the operation; but before she could answer, he repeated them himself. He also talked about the horrible witches he had seen on television: he seemed to imply that their frightening powers were like those of the surgeon he had endured.*

*It was evident that Gary was not bewildered by his being in an oxygen tent, nor did he look unknowingly upon his bandage. Later conversation also made clear that he had not found the operating room an entirely unfamiliar place: the strong lights, the masks, the green suits, the shiny instruments—all were much like the ones we looked at in the book and talked about.*

Gary recovered nicely from his operation and was discharged without delay. We can assume that the preparation had reassured the child and speeded his recovery. Usually, though, we would prefer to have a little more time to prepare a child.

Here is another report of a child's reaction to a serious operation, recorded by a medical student:

*Danny, ten, was admitted because of a severe injury to his right eye. Within a month it became certain that the eye would never heal properly. Enucleation was scheduled for the next afternoon, leaving little time to prepare the child for the loss of the eye.*

*On the morning of the operation, I asked Danny if Dr. M. (the ophthalmologist) had talked to him yet about the operation. He replied that the doctor had talked to both him and his mother separately, the night before.*

*"Did Dr. M. tell you what he plans to do during the operation?"*

*"Yes, he said they're going to 'line' my eye, or something like that, and they're going to make tracings of it."*

*"Did your mother tell you what the doctor had said to her?"*

*"She said they are going to fix my eye so I can see out of it again."*

*Knowing for a fact that Dr. M. had told them both that the eye would have to be removed, I then asked, "What will happen if the doctor can't fix your eye, Danny?"*

*In a most unconcerned tone, Danny replied, "Nothing will happen. I'll just have one good eye, that's all. I'll be One-eyed Danny, and that's that."*

*With this, he walked into the playroom, chuckling to himself.*

*For the remainder of the morning, Danny copied pictures from a book. His reproductions were quite good, except that all the people he drew showed large, saucer-like eyes. He appeared calm and almost heroically indifferent as he readied himself for his early-afternoon nap, though he did say, "I get scared every time the elevator bell rings because I think they're coming for me."*

*Upon awakening from his nap, Danny seemed to realize that the time for his operation was drawing near, because he began to stutter, talked in circles, and tugged nervously at his bed clothes. When the orderlies finally came, he inquired excitedly whether I was really going to go with him to the operating room. When I assured him that I was, he seemed somewhat relieved and asked the orderlies to hurry up so he could "get it over with."*

*When we stopped in the corridor outside the operating room, however, Danny wanted to know, in a frantic-sounding voice, what was going to happen, how long the operation would take, when he would be able to play again, if his eye would hurt, and so forth. Upon entering the operating room his questions abruptly ceased. It seemed as if the sight of the room had taken his breath away. Large beads of perspiration appeared on his forehead.*

*Satisfied that it would be a while before things would be in readiness for the surgeons, Danny relaxed and closed his functioning eye. This period of relaxation came to a sudden end, though, when the anesthesiologist introduced him to the sweet-smelling rubber mask. He grimaced severely, and as tears welled up in his eyes he cried, "No, no, not yet! Don't put me to sleep yet. Wait a while! Will I be able to see out of my eye when they're finished? Please, please don't put me to sleep! I'll never wake up again!"*

*The anesthesiologist withdrew the mask and waited until Danny had been reassured that the doctors would do what they thought best for him and that he would surely wake up again. Then as the mask descended upon him once more, Danny turned his head away and pleaded, "Why can't they operate when I'm awake?" A brief explanation that his operation would be a very painful one indeed if he were not asleep, temporarily convinced Danny. But it was only after he no longer had the necessary faculties to hold his breath that Danny gave in.*

It is obvious that Danny went through agonies just before surgery, in spite of the support the medical student gave him through his protective presence.

The time for preparing this boy was very short. Regardless, this type of operation will always be feared and experienced as a mutilation.

Our last example, reported by a third worker, concerns preparation for an operation involving less danger and damage, and a much shorter hospital stay. It shows how a pre-adolescent responded.

*Willie, twelve-years-old, had been admitted for circumcision and hernia repair two days prior to the operation. On the day before surgery, I took him aside and explained and showed him in great detail what would happen. Willie said nothing during my talk except when I showed him the panorama of the operating room, to which he exclaimed "Wow!" At this point, as well as at several other times, I emphasized how it is scary no matter how old you are, and that even adults don't like operations and are sort of frightened about it. I then drew details of the circumcision, saying that I want him to be sure that he knows just where the skin is that will be removed, because some boys if they aren't sure, worry about what will be cut off. In the playroom, he made no mention of the forthcoming operation.*

*Willie went to surgery the following morning. That afternoon as he returned from the recovery room, he asked the nurse if she would get me. He then told me what the operation was like, adding, "You forgot to tell me I'd have to wait outside the operating room." We talked a little more, and he offered me a piece of gum. The day following surgery, Willie participated fully in the playroom, and went home one day later.*

These three cases illustrate preparation without use of special standardized aids. However, now we have developed some of the latter. One is the set of outline drawings, some of which are reproduced in Appendix E. We have found them quite valuable both in the preparation of some children for surgery and for explanation of an internal illness.

Just recently we found a picture that used the same method. More than four centuries ago, Albrecht Dürer drew a self-portrait in the nude, on which he marked the spot where he felt pain, presumably to consult an out-of-town physician. The spot is in the area of the spleen, and it is believed that Dürer perhaps had spleen trouble resulting from malaria which he may have contracted on a trip to Italy.

A child often has distorted ideas about his illness and about what is being done to his body. A simple method of helping him is to offer accurate

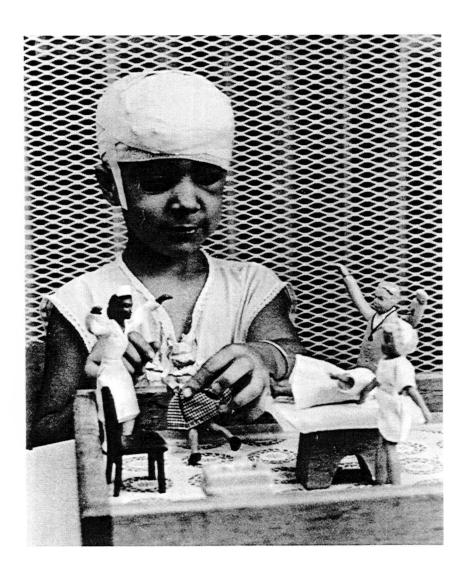

*After neurosurgery this absorbed six-year-old reenacts a bandage change.*

information about his body and the procedures to be done. Children of all ages can talk more freely and understand more clearly when a drawing is used as an adjunct to an explanation, and so can some adults. Spontaneous drawings or paintings by children also often show us their areas of concern or their misunderstandings. We can help a child better once we understand some of his fears.

Several good books have been published to help parents prepare their young child for a simple operation like tonsillectomy.[1] We have found them wanting in details for other operations and felt that the children should have an active part in using a book that prepares them for what they have to expect. Two of my co-workers have produced just such a book. A third one wrote a story which will be found in Appendix D. Written in the language of the pre-adolescent, it is meant to be read by the older children themselves.

It also works well to read a story about a child's experience in the hospital to a group of children. Some have had their surgery already and some will be having it. The children who have had an operation usually have many comments about how they felt and what happened. In a group it is often easier for children to ask questions and many are reassured by hearing of the experiences of other children. But it also offers the adult a chance in the lively discussion to pick up and correct some of the more fearful misconceptions children have. One thing we often find mentioned is that doctors and nurses have masks on so that they would not have to smell "that awful stuff." It also becomes clear that the masked adult is often taken for a villain who hides his face to cover up his evil intentions. Seeing children after surgery who are up and around and function well also helps to diminish some fears.

Our playroom equipment includes bandages, an old rubber mask, plaster of paris and stockinette to make a cast for a doll, paper, nurses' caps, surgical gloves, a real stethoscope, and syringes. We also have a plastic intravenous set-up made from lotion bottles and tubing that can be attached to a doll buggy. Aside from the child's handling or playing with this equipment the nurse or playroom worker may use it to demonstrate a procedure on a doll.

If there is little time for preparation, particularly in elective minor surgery, a set of pictures depicting the steps prior to and immediately following surgery are helpful. We use illustrations of the preoperative

[1] See Bibliography

injection, the move to surgery, receiving anesthesia, waking in the recovery room where one sees I.V.'s running (intravenous infusions, hereafter referred to by the usual designation, I.V.) or an oxygen tent, and finally back in one's own room awake and with mother's soothing presence.

Let me add an example of an unusual preparation for a supposedly minor procedure, an electroencephalogram. It shows the empathy and creativity of my former co-worker Ruth Coggins Horwood. I quote from her notes:

Jeff was 6 years old at the time of his admission to the hospital for an evaluation. He had become increasingly unmanageable and his unpredictable outbursts of anger were frightening. There was also concern over what appeared to be "autistic behavior." The many motions he made with his body, especially with his hands, were bizarre. He related poorly to people. His speech was parrot-like and repetitious.

One part of the evaluation consisted of an electroencephalogram (EEG). The first two attempts at EEG were unsuccessful due to Jeff's frantic behavior. Sedatives given seemed to stimulate. Larger doses would have interfered with the results of the test. The child was generating annoyance, anger, and fear in the adults working with him.

How could I help Jeff understand what would happen? How could I enlist cooperation from him? I was aware of his ability to read. Did the printed word convey meaning to him? I ventured to find out. I sat down with him at a table and wrote in large bold letters "Miss Coggins and Jeff are going for a walk. We will just look. We will come back." We were silent during that short trip. We just looked. When we returned, Jeff sat down beside me and watched intently as I wrote each word of the following story, illustrating it by line drawings:

### A BOOK ABOUT JEFF'S TRIP TO EEG

Jeff went for a walk with Miss Coggins. They peeked into a room. A lady showed Jeff a machine which was making lines on long pieces of paper.

A man was resting on the table. The man was being very quiet. He did not need to cry. There were no needles. No shots. No one hurt the man. The man felt sleepy.

Today Jeff will have some medicine to make him sleepy. Jeff will lie down in his bed. Miss Coggins and Jeff will look at books. Miss Coggins will read to Jeff. Jeff will read to Miss Coggins.

Jeff will soon feel sleepy. After a while Jeff will take a ride in his bed to visit the room where the lady showed him the machine. Miss Coggins will go with Jeff. Jeff will not be alone.

Jeff will lie on another bed. The lady will not hurt Jeff. No needles. No shots. Jeff will not need to cry. The lady will put little bits of paste on Jeff's hair. It will not hurt.

Wire will go from Jeff's hair to the machine. The machine will not hurt Jeff. Jeff will need to be quiet. Jeff will not wiggle. Jeff will feel sleepy.

After a while Jeff will go back up the elevator. Miss Coggins will stay with Jeff. Then Jeff will see the playroom. Jeff will see his friends. Jeff will see Max the pet hamster. Jeff will be happy. Jeff's Mommy will come.

The story was read by the boy many times that morning. We then went down to the EEG unit. An appropriate page would be held up for Jeff to read at the first sign of agitation in the minutes preceding the test. He was able to control his body and eventually dozed briefly and the test could be completed. It was a small medical victory but a significant victory for Jeff who looked very happy in response to the praise given him.

Our belief in the value of preparation is hard to validate. It is difficult to show how a child would have reacted after a different type of preparation, or with none at all. One case in which we received a testimonial, as it were, was that of a four-year-old girl with whom we had done very careful preparation for a leg amputation. It took some time to convince the desperate parents of the necessity of letting the little girl know that she would return from surgery without one of her legs. Eleven months after the amputation Ruthie had to return for a stump revision. It went very smoothly. The mother turned to me while waiting for her child and said: "You know, I am so grateful that we and the hospital staff told Ruthie about the amputation last year before it happened. I would never have been able to get her back to the hospital otherwise, because she asked me, 'Will they cut my other leg off?' and when I said, 'No, they will just work on your stump,' she trusted me."[2]

The situations in which this can be so plainly stated are, of course, rare. One is therefore tempted to demonstrate what happens with and without preparation by using material not written for the purpose. The Irish writer Sean O'Casey describes in his autobiography how as a child suffering from an eye disease he was taken to the ophthalmologist's clinic:

*Suddenly they found themselves in the doctor's room, and a nurse made them sit down on a special bench to wait for Mr. Story. It was a room full of a frightening light, for the whole north wall was a window from side to side, and from floor to ceiling. There was a ceaseless sound of instruments being taken from trays and being put back again. Tinkle, tinkle, tinkle, they went, and cold sweat formed on Johnny's brow. All round the wall*

[2] See Bibliography, Plank and Horwood.

*terrible pictures of diseases of the eye and ear were hanging. A nurse, in a blue calico dress, with narrow white stripes, was hurrying here and there, attending to the doctors; and everywhere there was a feeling of quiet, broken by a man's moan, or by a child's cry, that made Johnny tense his body with resentment and resistance.*

*...Johnny was led over to the window, and the bandage taken from his eyes: the light, the light, the cursed, blasted blinding light! He was seated on a chair; he was fixed between the doctor's legs; his head was bent back as far as a head can go; he could feel the doctor's fingers pressing into his cheek just below his eyes: the light, the light, the cursed, blasted, blinding light!*

*Open your eyes, said Story, and look out of the window; go on, open your eyes, like a good little boy.*

*—Open your eyes for the doctor, Johnny, said his mother.*

*—Open your eyes, said Story, sharply, open your eyes, at once, sir.*

*But the cursed, blasted, blinding light flooded pain in through the lids, and he kept them tightly closed. His mother nervously shook his arm.*

*—Open your eyes, you young rascal, she said.*

*But he sat, stiff, firm, and silent, and kept them closed.*

*—Story beckoned to two students. One of them held his head from behind the chair, the other held his arms, but still, firm, and silent, he kept them closed. His obstinacy forced them into fierceness; they took him out of the chair, while his mother, embarassed, threatened him with all sorts of violence when she got him home. They stretched him, on his back, froglike, on the floor, students holding his legs, nurses holding his arms, while Story, kneeling beside him, pressed his fingers under his eyes firmly and gently, till with an exasperated yell, Johnny was forced to open them, and Story, from a tiny glass container, instantly injected into his eyes a tiny stream of what looked like cold water, which spread like a cooling balm over the burning ulcerated surface of his eyeballs.*

The conclusion to be drawn from this childhood memory is obvious, but our examples show also that preparation for surgery may have varying degrees of success and may produce different results with different children. We must not think that any child who has been properly prepared will go into surgery like a lamb while an unprepared child will not. The very opposite may be true: the unprepared child, not knowing what to expect—in fact, not expecting anything—may show little outward excitement or may be frozen into obedience. But his later reaction may be severe. The value of good preparation for an operation appears afterwards, in the speed of recuperation and in freedom from neurotic symptoms.

# 4/Working Through Feelings After Surgery

Children's reactions after surgery vary greatly. Some youngsters may remain fearful and passive long after the physical discomforts have disappeared. Others will function like their old selves in a short time, while a third group may reverse the roles and change from the submissive part they had to follow as surgery patients to an aggressive one during convalescence.

We are all familiar with the adult who returns from the hospital and recounts tales and details of his hospitalization time and again, as if to detoxify its frightening aspects. Children have the same need but are much less able to tell spontaneously about their experiences. They need the opportunity for repetition, in dramatic play and in words, to allow them to go over the events that troubled them. This play can take on different forms and can give us good indications of whether a child is reacting to a past trauma normally or with fixed anxiety. In the examples that follow we will describe children who represent these types.

## THE FEARFUL, PASSIVE CHILD

Some children come from surgery or some other procedures so frightened that they seem almost frozen into inactivity. They are not only unable to tell about or play out the traumatic experience, but they stop playing altogether. The younger the child, the more often do we see such passivity and grief.

Two-and-a-half-year-old Ann was admitted for removal of an enlarged cervical lymph node. Though shy at first, she opened up to be a happy playroom participant, active and talkative for her age. About a week after admission she had her operation. She spent most of the following day in her cubicle. When she came to the playroom two days postoperatively, she seemed to be a changed little girl. She just stood there, looking sad, and was not interested in any of the toys offered her. This went on most of the morning. The worker then brought a plastic syringe and a cup of water, showed Ann how it worked, and left it in front of her. After looking at it suspiciously first, she then played with it in an absorbed way. The following day she again looked sad and did not participate. We talked to her, saying how nice it was that her operation was all over and that she would be going home soon. We asked if she would like to play with the syringe again. She didn't reply, but when we brought it she picked it up almost immediately, played with it and then switched easily to another activity and was her old self.

Seven-year-old Margaret was listless the day after her tonsillectomy and did not feel well enough to get out of bed. We moved her bed close to a group of playing children, but she remained sad and aloof. The worker thought that she might show her the drawing of the operating room that she had shown her before her operation. She brought the picture and asked Margaret if the room where she had had her operation looked like that. The child kept looking at the picture while the worker was called to the phone and after she returned. When Margaret finally put the picture down, the worker asked her if she would like to paint. Margaret said yes and painted steadily for the next hour. Here the visual confrontation with a trauma passed seemed to have broken the spell.

## THE ACTIVE ONES

Eleven-year-old Mary was hospitalized for a tonsillectomy. Her mother had prepared her well. The child participated fully in the playroom before surgery and was back the day after her operation. We noticed her playing with a doll on a model surgery cart, giving an injection. We asked what was the matter with the doll. Mary replied, "She is in the hospital for her tonsillectomy and I have to give her a shot." Mary then covered the doll, wheeled the cart around the room, walked over to the toy telephone and said: "Your daughter is all finished with her operation, and she did fine, and she will be right down." This is certainly a wholesome reaction, though on a younger level than we would expect it if the child had not been sick.

We saw another example of spontaneously playing out a traumatic event

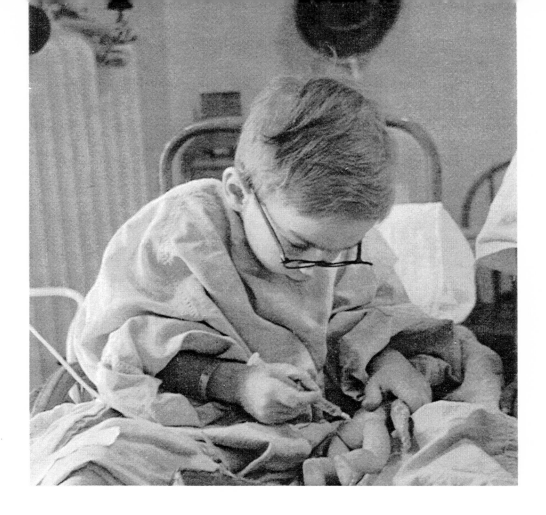

*Still in his wheelchair, dressed in a surgeon's gown, Peter gives an injection to a doll. If children can work through their feelings while they are still raw, they can master them.*

in five-year-old Terry. This little boy was known to all of us for his numerous admissions as a patient who had hemophilia. He usually came to the hospital following trauma such as a fall or too much vigorous wrestling. He would need intravenous medication for several days and ice packs often had to be applied to the affected area. We have medical and surgical equipment available for play. It consists of an I.V. stand and plastic bottle and tubing, plastic syringes, tape, surgical masks, gowns, tongue blades, three-way stop-cock, and a doll-sized rubber water bottle. Usually Terry spent at least half a day with this equipment. He reproduced on a doll the treatment he had experienced. He put cold packs to the affected area and started the I.V. in the correct place. One incident showed us how important the precision and the details of the play were to him. He worked intently with complete concentration, saying little. However, that day he had an intricate I.V. setup, with stop-cock and water, attached to a doll's arm. He complained to the worker that it wasn't running. She answered jokingly, "Maybe you don't have it in the vein." Terry looked up and said, very seriously, "I know I got it in a good vein and if anybody touches it I am going to be furious with him." With great determination he went ahead to adjust the tubing until it worked properly.

We think that children who can play so freely and talk about painful procedures will be less likely to be frightened later by memories of the hospital experience. Playing helps them prophylactically.

THE HYPER-AGGRESSIVE CHILDREN

These are usually young boys after an operation or children who had previously to submit to painful situations of an emotional or physical nature. Their belligerence seems to put a protective shield around them so that no more danger can come their way.

Billy, who illustrates this type, had been hospitalized for dog bites. We were told that he had inadvertently kicked his dog which then attacked the eleven-year-old boy quite viciously. During his seven days of hospitalization Billy was constantly aggressive both in word and action. One night he sneaked into the treatment room, took a syringe, filled it with water, and disturbed the sleeping children by using it as a water gun. When the nurse tried to stop him he squirted her, too. His parents described him as a well adjusted child prior to the accident—we saw a very upset youngster who took on the role of the aggressor, who unexpectedly hurt others, just as it had happened to him in playing with his dog.

It is likely that withdrawn children like Margaret and Ann would, in the course of time, again have become able to play on their own without the help in the playroom. However, it seems that we could shorten the time of anxiety after the operation by recognizing that their first activities had to be related to the traumatic event. Diversion with these children did not work.

Only after they had cautiously moved into activity by handling something that had brought pain and fear to them previously were they able to return to the normal childlike play.

## WORKING THROUGH AFTER A SERIOUS OPERATION
The case of Ruthie whom we mentioned in the preceding chapter taught us how a very serious operation—a leg amputation—could be worked through with a little girl and how it involved the cooperation of all professions to achieve it. The observations made in the playroom illustrate how four-year-old Ruthie was able to come to grips with her loss and the procedures applied to her. It points out how observant a worker must be to pick up the child's leads.

Ruthie had come to the hospital with meningococcemia. After a stormy acute episode, gangrene set in on her legs and it gradually became evident that a partial amputation would be necessary. We mentioned the paper describing the preparation of the parents and the child in the preceding chapter.

Here we would like to describe in detail how the working through was accomplished. We faced two major problems. One, we had to help not only the child, but also her family and the staff to accept the loss of a leg. Two, the process of healing is a slow and painful one after amputation. The child had to face skin grafts and stump revisions as well as a long period of waiting for the prosthesis to be made and adjusted on her stump.

This little girl responded very well to opportunities to talk about what happened to her and how hard it was to wait for her new leg. Since she had learned to trust us, we could reassure her that the prosthesis would come as soon as the wound had healed sufficiently. We saw how she needed to deny some strong wishes in order to cope with her exasperation for having to wait so long. "I don't want to walk," she would say. We reassured her that we understood how hard it was to wait. Ruth was also able to answer other children's questions about her leg: "It was sick, and the doctor took it off."

One little incident shows how everything is brought into relation with the traumatic experience that needs working through. One day, a split-thickness skin graft, taken from the abdomen, was placed on her leg. It was necessary to apply cast that fully covered both legs. The next day as we were playing with some sea shells, pointing to one where the outer part had been chipped off, Ruth said: "It has no skin." This was the opening for discussing her skin graft with her.

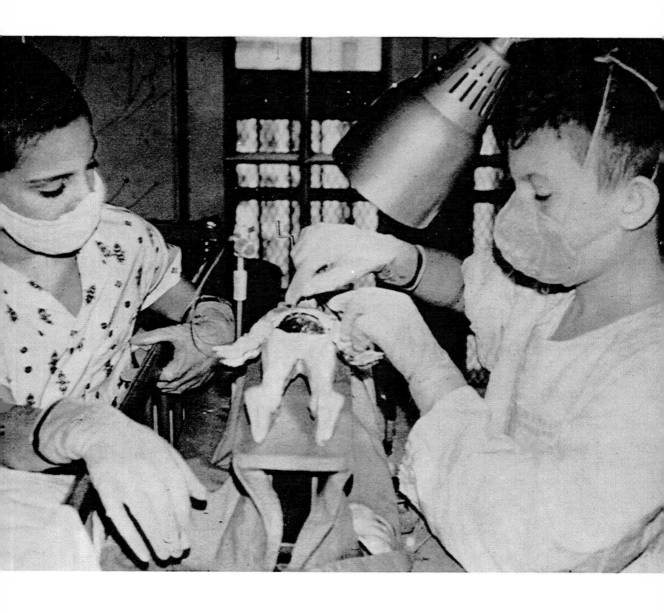

*Masked and gloved like surgeons, children "operate"; the transfusion apparatus is built from construction toys.*

In addition to the playthings mentioned before, our playroom contains some authentic surgery equipment which is only used in select cases under close adult supervision. It consists of an I.V. set up, surgical drapes, caps and masks, a (dull) knife, and a mask for anesthesia. (We followed the selection suggested in Florence Erickson's monograph.[1])

Ruthie became very interested in this equipment, and she and a girl of eight performed multiple operations on the dolls, with the older one taking the role of the chief surgeon. Ruthie's operations were almost exclusively leg surgery. In addition to other procedures, all primarily on the legs, she frequently gave injections into the soles of the doll's feet, taped the doll's legs together, and sometimes handcuffed the doll before performing an operation. This play was only terminated when the playroom closed and began again the first thing the next day. The term "play" does not really fit here; it was an activity fully absorbing the child's emotional and intellectual capacities.

Another incident shows Ruthie's struggle with the loss of her leg. One day a nursing student was painting a large Santa Claus on a window. It happened that the perspective made one leg appear shorter than the other. Ruthie asked the nursing student, "Why is one leg shorter? Did they cut it off, or did you just forget to put it on?" Another time in the playroom she told how soft the new skin felt that was growing back on her leg, and took a worker's finger to touch it.

We had a chance to see how the child's working through had succeeded during a home visit five months after Ruthie's discharge. She moved around the house with a noticeably abnormal gait but with extreme agility. She even climbed stairs, wearing regular oxford shoes. Her mother told us that she loved to be outdoors and was learning to rollerskate and ride a bicycle. Ruth will start to go to kindergarten on a regular schedule.

We believe that it was the stabilizing presence of the child-care worker and her feeling for the child that allowed Ruth to play out her concerns. The surgery equipment alone would not have changed the frightening, passive experience of the operation into an activity which could absorb the child's anxiety.

# 5/If Death Occurs
## on a Children's Ward

To the kindly adult, concerned to protect children from worries about themselves, particularly while they are in the hospital, it would seem most important to cover up everything which might frighten them. How strange then, that we advocate that children should be told of the death of a child if it occurs on their ward.

Death on the children's ward has many implications for the other children, though an onlooker may not realize that they are being affected by it. The protective screen of pretending not to know what people, on whom one depends, don't want one to know, often works well at the time but may backfire later. The fear never to return home is part of every child's hospital experience, even if it is not expressed in words.

It may, at first glance, seem logical and kinder to try to cover up the fact that death occurs. Shouldn't one rather tell children, if they ask about a patient, that he went home or was transferred to another ward? This may be an acceptable way out for the adult who himself has deep feelings at a child's death. No good nurse, doctor or child-care worker can take care of a child without a sense of loss and futility (and maybe irrational guilt) when his care could not prolong life or when tragedy strikes. Therefore, it is only natural if the adult wants to return to his daily work and not to be reminded of the loss himself.

What in children's psychological makeup makes it desirable for them to know or to ignore the fact of death? Children always observe and sense situations which adults wish and believe they did not see. Invariably they sense the strained and sinister, and if not helped to clarify what they think happened, the adults' silence may increase their fears in fantasy, rather than spare them sorrow.

To deny the existence of danger may be helpful for keeping up defenses against unmanageable anxieties. But the anxieties can become overwhelming if the professional worker through his silence overlooks a child's need to be reassured about himself and his future.

Children's reactions to death are highly individual. And so are the circumstances under which death may occur in a hospital. We can best discuss how one may handle such difficult situations by bringing some examples from our experience. They will show how different children manage to cope with their fears, sadness or fantasies about death, and how doctors, nurses and child-care workers could help.

Maxine, age twelve, isolated in a room with severe burns, said angrily when she saw a boy wheeled by her room on a cart, "Oh, he is probably going for an operation and he might even die. They never tell you anything that's going on around here." When asked what she meant, she mentioned the death of a child whom she had never seen and whose bed had been several rooms away from hers. We had not thought it warranted at the time to tell her, but news of this kind "travels through the bush." From then on we let the oldest children know by talking to them individually if a child had died.

Two little sisters, Maria, age eleven, and Lucia, age nine, came to the hospital after having been hit by a car as they crossed the street. Lucia never regained consciousness. Maria, with a fractured hip and many bruises, was too ill and confused to notice what was going on. Lucia died after a day but Maria started to respond to her environment and asked where she was and what had happened to her and her sister.

The parents, trying hard to keep up a cheerful front, told her that her sister was at home playing. Though the hospital staff had full understanding of the parents' need to spare the child and to keep their own anxiety under control by bypassing questions, we worried about Maria. Jointly, doctor, nurse and child-care workers decided that as soon as Maria was completely out of danger she should be told the truth.

Since the parents were still so overwhelmed by their loss, it was planned that the doctor would start telling Maria of her sister's death in the parents' presence. Maria cried hard and asked many questions which could be answered reassuringly. She called each of us, nurses and child-care workers as we passed her bed, to tell us about the tragedy. She wondered if Lucia would see Saint Peter in Heaven. She expressed real sadness that her only sister was dead. We could reassure her that Lucia had not suffered, which Maria easily understood, as she could not remember anything after having been hit by the car. She ate heartily for the first time and rapidly became talkative and interested in people and activities. Time and again Maria would talk to one of the child-care workers about how lonely it was for her parents at home.

In this case the child could spontaneously talk about the accident and her feeling about being the one who was saved, while her emotional reactions were still very fluid. The parents, terribly hurt by the loss, did not talk much with Maria but reassured her by showing their love and concern for her. Most of the working-through came spontaneously during the play periods, facilitated through the child's confidence in our staff. When after many weeks of hospitalization, the return home became a reality, Maria had another upsurge of worry and grief. Again, these feelings could be handled by the staff, and the child was well prepared for her return home as the only girl in the family.

In contrast to Maria, where we had to undo a confusing statement, little Louise illustrated how the clinical team that anticipated a child's death could plan ahead what to tell the other children on the ward.

Fourteen-month-old Louise had had muscle weakness and respiratory deficiency since birth (amyotonia congenita). Since she had to be in a respirator she was hospitalized in our Respirator Care and Rehabilitation Center. These children have tremendous anxieties about their own life and some of them have witnessed death during their hospital stay. Seeing the resulting anxieties we wanted to do right by the children this time.

The team decided that little Louise should be in a room by herself and if she died the other children should be told as soon as possible and not learn about it through the grapevine. We decided who should talk to the children, planning for every time sector during the day. We felt that the doctor they all knew best was the obvious person. The chief resident was our first choice, and it was he who was on duty when little Louise died in a side room one evening around bed time. Since we had time to think about the other children ahead of time, we were prepared as to what to tell them and how to soothe their fears.

We stressed the following facts:

Louise was different from them. She had a different illness, not polio. Did the children remember how she could not swallow and had to be fed through a tube? How she could not sit up or be out of the respirator for any length of time? None of these things were true for them now—they had gotten better. What impressed our chief resident most when he talked to the children individually that night were the varied attitudes to the news of Louise's death. Gregory, age eight, acted as if this was sensational news (he was the most frightened boy on the ward, who had been in a respirator during his first weeks of illness next to a child who died.) Denise (age six) expressed her fears by crying but yet could be reassured through talking with the doctor about little Louise and how she had liked her. Claire (age six) was equally frightened but tried to deny it by changing the subject immediately. She was the sickest child and needed constant artificial respiration to stay alive. Peter (age eight) asked the doctor many intelligent and factual questions and was reassured and satisfied by the answers. For a long time after the event, the children referred to the side room where Louise had died as "Louise's room."

This enumeration of reactions exemplifies what we can expect in different children: denial in those who are most frightened about their illness, like Gregory and Claire, unhappiness, but a working-through of fears in children who are equally handicapped but can face realities a little better. These children had parents who had been better able to cope with their own child's illness and had helped them to face facts. A strong bond remained between the children and their doctor.

When a young child who may conceivably die during hospitalization brings up the question of the possibility of his own death, we reassure him with great conviction and help the child in his attempts to deny the possibility. We would never try to prepare a child for his own death; however, we would facilitate his expression of thoughts and anxieties. The report on Betty shows how this was done.

Betty was a five-year-old whom we had known for over a year during recurrent hospitalizations for a Wilm's Tumor (a cancerous growth). She usually came to the hospital very weak with severe leg pains which made it impossible for her to walk. After a few days in bed, receiving intravenous medication, she was an active little girl again, wanting to be in the playroom. Her favorite play was to be mother or nurse to a doll. Some days the doll got bathed and dressed for dinner, and some days the dolly was too sick. Betty wrapped bandages around the doll's abdomen. "You are sick," we overheard her say. "What are you going to do for her?" the worker asked. "She's got to stay in bed and get an I.V.; then she can get up and play." "Umhum, and what are you planning for her?" "Well, she's not gonna die, if that's what you mean," she indignantly informed the worker. "Oh, that's good. You know how to make her well." Betty went about her nursing, singing as she put the doll to bed. When Betty was admitted the next time she had to be confined to bed with an I.V. again. She asked for her doll, which she tucked in beside her.

Sally (age nine) was hospitalized at the same time and liked little Betty very much. She was assigned for special observations to a medical student. We are quoting from his notes:

*Somehow Sally learned that her friend had cancer and subsequently began to flood me with questions about it. Without going into any morbid details, I explained as best I could the nature of the rapidly dividing cancer cells.*

*Betty died a few days later, and, Sally unfortunately was witness to the excitement attending that event. Two or three days passed before Sally felt free to discuss what was troubling her:*

*"Betty really died, didn't she, doctor?"*

*"Yes, Sally, she did. Betty had a different kind of sickness than any of the rest of the children have here. The doctors couldn't help her get better, like they helped you and Jimmy and Sam and the others."*

*"She had cancer, didn't she?"*

*"Yes, one of the most serious kinds of cancer."*

*"Do you think I'll have a baby when I'm big?"*

*"It's quite possible. Why do you ask?"*

*"Well, babies start out real small inside you and grow bigger and bigger, don't they? Just like cancer does. What's the difference between having a baby and having a cancer?"*

*It was no small task to answer this child's profound question, but it was well worth the time and effort required to do so. This conversation certainly showed how active children's thinking is while they are forced into inactivity through illness and how their thoughts encompass everything that matters to them—from conception to death. But it also shows that there is often a delay before a question of great importance to the child is asked. It took Sally several days to ask her doctor.*

How to help older terminally ill children with their feelings is an especially difficult question. They generally know that they are "not supposed to know," they tend to deny the severity of their illness so as to be able to live with it, and yet they desperately want our honesty.

We must listen to them with more than the ordinary attention. This is not as easy as it sounds, as in just these situations, where privacy and serenity would be most desired for a conversation, obstacles present themselves most intrusively. We must explore whether some of these hindrances are not within ourselves. I wish that I could say more or that I could bring examples as moving as those of the reaction to the death of others, but perhaps we can comfort ourselves with the thought that if we can lead the child to feel that we don't bypass him, that we are with him to share his burden, we have not altogether failed him.

I think that our case material illustrates one essential point. Children build their defenses to protect themselves from too much pain, but they also want to know the truth. The role of the adult is not to help to erect these defenses through silence or untruth, but to recognize them when the child uses them and to keep the bridge to reality open.

If a child who died was well known and suffered the same illness, the need to deny or to bypass the thoughts about death may be most essential and necessary to preserve the other children's will for recovery. One should be very cautious when and how to mention the death. But even under these circumstances it is important to find an occasion to tell children about it.

Denial may still occur and should be left undisturbed, as it serves a protective function. The important thing is that the child know that he can trust the adults' honesty and ask questions when he wants to. Reassurance is particularly helpful if it comes from those who know about illness and administer treatments to make the children well again.

Different ways will have to be found each time depending on the circumstances. Our case material shows the great variety of situations a professional team has to face and plan for.

# 6/Play and Activities

Children who are sick or convalescent need special planning for their activities and their play. In this chapter we want to discuss what to watch for in working with infants, children on bed rest, children with restricted motion, and children in isolation. These groups differ sufficiently from other groups of children at play or in school to need understanding of their specific difficulties and of the special equipment required. The child-care worker does not find a precedent in other settings.

We will also discuss activities which fit hospitalized children in general and which seem particularly suited to create an atmosphere of ease in which children can live a childlike life on the ward in spite of personal adversity.

Readers looking for a detailed description of techniques for activities successful on a children's ward may consult Appendix A. There we shall also suggest sources of supplies.

## INFANTS
Infants past about ten months should be included in a playroom program. The primary consideration should be to comfort these babies by holding them often, to talk to them and keep them active, or to prop them up so that they can watch what goes on and what others are doing. Our main concern is to counteract the feeling of deep loss any baby of that age experiences through separation from the mother. The infants can be held for feeding or while playing. A change of environment away from the crib is stimulating in itself and encourages babies to move. They enjoy playing on a mat, moving in a walker, or being in a rocker or a baby swing. They also love having an adult play with them while they are in their crib. A ball about two

inches in diameter can be suspended in a crocheted net across the crib for the child to push with his hands or feet, or a baby gym can be hung across. We found some children enjoy blowing at mobiles attached to the crib and watching the movement. Rattling toys and wind-up music boxes have great appeal. Both infants and toddlers who are ambulatory enjoy sitting in small enclosures. They seem to feel secure in an enclosed space like a wooden box on the floor. Another favorite activity is water play. The children also enjoy a box of sawdust to put their hands in or which they can shovel; large wooden blocks to stand on and carry, push or pull-toys which are not too noisy, and the always-loved soft toys round out the basic collection.

BED REST

Bed rest may be ordered for a variety of reasons. The rest seldom needs to be so restricting that the child can not use his hands, eyes and ears for quiet activities. In each case, the clinical team must decide on the degree of rest. Permitting limited activities often results in more rest because the child relaxes and stops resisting the restriction.

One way to interrupt the confinement of the bed is to carry the child to a low canvas cot in the playroom. This change of environment is refreshing in itself. There the child can watch other children or listen to records or stories. Since the cot is narrow, the child's movement is automatically restricted. Similarly we lift children onto a low push cart with sides which is large enough for a child to lie in. In the cart, they can easily be moved from place to place.

Many activities can be adapted to bed rest. For all "messy" ones the child should wear a rubber apron (it can be made from hospital sheeting) and the bedding should be protected by a rubber sheet. Children of all ages enjoy water play. The younger ones like sailing boats and floating animals, the older ones washing dishes or bathing dolls.

Sand or sawdust in wooden boxes (14 by 20 inches with 4-inch sides) makes an excellent medium for maneuvering small animal or human figures. Spoons and toy dishes add ideas for play.

The child on bed rest can paint, finger-paint or paste. One sheet of paper can be taped to the rack of an over-the-bed table or to a tray with legs, folding the legs under on one side so that the tray slopes at an angle towards the child, or to a special rack. The rack made by our carpenters has two broad sturdy legs which rest on the bed on each side of the child's body. The rack itself, a flat surface with a ledge at the bottom, is attached to the legs by screws. When the screws are loosened the rack can be tilted. Slots in the legs allow the screws to slide up and down to adjust the height of the rack.

Manipulating magnetic numbers or counting symbols on a magnet board is fun. Children also enjoy playing with figures which stick to a flannel board.

Younger children like running cars, wooden trains or "walking animals" down inclined boards from an over-the-bed table or tray to the bed.

A light-weight doll house for the bed can be made by cutting off one side of a cardboard box and painting the inside to resemble a room.

RESTRICTED MOTION

Children who have one arm restricted by traction or an I.V. can still enjoy most activities in bed. They may particularly like hand and finger puppets or a glove with a different face on each finger.

Pasting cutouts is fun. The child can apply the paste to the sheet of paper which has been taped to a tray or rack instead of to the cutout figure.

Paper dolls already cut out are popular. These can be taped to an inclined tray or leaned against the tray. Scotch tape can be used to temporarily attach the dolls' clothes. Make two rings of tape about one inch in diameter. Flatten the rings and stick them to the doll. Touch the protruding sticky side several times until it is less adhesive. The tape ring will hold the doll's clothes on, but they can easily be replaced by a new outfit.

As a special treat for little ones, a "feel box" may be prepared. (Children with eyes bandaged or in a respirator are especially pleased.) Use a cigar box or shoe box and put in it all sorts of tiny objects which are interesting to touch or smell. (Remember in making selections, that some things also feel good enough to taste.) A feather, smooth stones, small figures, sea shells, pine cones, a pillow filled with rose petals or balsam, keys, a rabbit tail, and miniature toys such as those found in cereal boxes are some things children enjoy discovering. Older ones may like to run a record player. Small pets at the bedside add a special quality.

ISOLATION

Children in isolation need toys for stimulation and expression, even more than others. The choice is limited though to things which can be washed with alcohol and aired after use, or discarded, but there are still a host of possibilities. The contact with others is unfortunately very limited, so things have to substitute for people. Older children take an interest in things which they make to decorate their rooms. These can be made with paper, scissors, crayons, liquid paint (in paper cups) as well as chalk. (Look for craft techniques in Appendix A.) The youngsters like riddles, number and cross-word puzzles as well as other mental games found in children's magazines. Boys like to learn to tie knots. Games like jacks, pick-up-sticks and cards can interest these children. Radio or television brings much enjoyment.

DRAMATIC PLAY AND MUSIC

Materials for dramatic play are one of the most important properties of the playroom. They include: dress-up clothes (particularly hats, bags, jackets, and skirts), a small suitcase, hand and finger puppets, dolls, housekeeping equipment, and a baby buggy either sturdy enough to hold a two-to four-year-old, or too small for them to get into. Small plastic animals and men (particularly cowboys and Indians with horses, soldiers, and families), toy cars and trucks, a furnished doll house (the bathroom and bedroom furniture will be the most popular), a doctor or nurse set containing a syringe and a real stethoscope, and a mirror on the wall are also useful.

It is most rewarding to see a frightened little boy smile for the first time as he sees himself dressed up like a cowboy with a gun, or to watch a shy little girl tenderly feeding her doll. She may talk to the doll when she is afraid to speak to anyone else. The child with a crocodile puppet on his hand lets the puppet say things he himself couldn't say, or try to bite people. Animal puppets seem to allow children freedom of aggressive expression almost better than human puppets. A child with one arm in a cast or strapped to an intravenous board will enjoy a set of finger puppets which fit over the fingers of his free hand.

Toy animals and people and the doll house allow children to imagine being someone else who is stronger and better able to protect himself. They may reenact reassuring family scenes or frightening hospital experiences and express their hostility. It is often difficult for a child to accept treatment, but if he plays the role of doctor or nurse, giving the treatment himself, he feels better. A frightened child may even be afraid to handle a syringe at first. Before long, though, he will examine it, see how it works, and next give shots to all the dolls; or he will pretend to give injections to other children, his nurse, the doctor, or the child-care worker.

A toy suitcase is almost always in use. Children hurriedly fill it with trucks, blocks, or dress-up clothes and announce that they are going home. Or they pack all the doll's belongings and start on a trip with dollie in the buggy.

We find children examining themselves seriously in the wall mirror hung at their level, particularly if they are concerned as to what the illness may have done to them.

A punching bag is a good outlet for aggression. It is "dramatic" enough to be mentioned here, though we use it mostly outdoors.

Boys, particularly those with eye injuries who can not watch well and are handicapped in making things, are drawn to rhythmical instruments and music. The rhythm of the bongo drum attracted every older boy confined through his illness. The autoharp is a challenge to learn for children who have a longer hospital stay.

The effect of musical and rhythmical activities is obvious and fast. These activities help to establish pre-adolescents in a group and give them status.

## WATER, SAND, AND SAWDUST

Water play is a natural for almost all children. The shy and frightened children as well as the aggressive ones are attracted to it and spend much time repeating their play over and over. The very young ones like to pour a small amount of water from a pitcher into cups and pans. They are also fascinated to move ice cubes from one container into another either with their hands or a spoon. Slightly older children wash dishes, doll clothes, dolls, and particularly the doll's hair. Little boys enjoy sailing boats and floating animals. Bed-bound children use a flat-bottomed, high-sided dishpan with only one or two inches of water in the same way. Blowing soap bubbles delights many children.

Sand or sawdust in a wooden box makes an excellent platform for maneuvering small animals, vehicles, and people. These toys transform the sand or sawdust into a medium for dramatic play. Spoons or toy shovels and pans add play ideas.

Patting, shoveling, and pouring sand or sawdust seems to be as satisfying as water play. Sawdust is easier to clean up when spilled than sand. Children can be in any position while playing with these materials.

## LIVE ANIMALS AND PLANTS

Children, bed-bound or up, enjoy observing and caring for animals and plants. Goldfish, guppies, or water snails are easy to raise. Guppies and snails propagate, which fascinates children. Bed-bound children often ask for a fish in a bowl to care for at their bedside. One boy noticed which fish "woke up" first, and another discovered a variation in the markings of a mother guppie and watched to see if the offspring would have the same markings. Turtles, insect cocoons, tadpoles, and a bird feeder also interrupt the sterility of hospital living.

Hospital research divisions or a local zoo sometimes have hamsters, rabbits, white mice, and various amphibia and reptiles for the children, and can provide cages and pet food. We have raised generations of white mice on our wards.

Seeds of beans, lentils, or pumpkins can be grown on moist cotton in a cut-off milk carton at a child's bedside.

## BOOKS, MAGAZINES AND NEWSPAPERS

Libraries often make regular rounds loaning books to patients. Even if this service is available, it is good to have a basic library on hand. In selecting books, content as well as external features must be considered.

When youngsters are worried or in discomfort, they can concentrate for only short periods. They usually prefer books with easier reading than they ordinarily read.

Children who are ill like to identify in fantasy with someone who also has a struggle. *Madeline*, the story of a little French girl who gets her appendix out, *The Ugly Duckling*, and *The Little Engine That Could* are examples.

Since there are constantly new books available we don't want to give a list here but rather suggest certain points to consider in their choice. Here we are thinking mostly of older children who read to themselves. They like to identify with people who are strong and daring and have come through adversities. Nine-year-old Charlie may illustrate our point:

He was acutely ill with the Guillain-Barré syndrome, a neurologic disease similar in its manifestations to poliomyelitis. He had to be tube fed, was in an iron lung and had a tracheotomy. No wonder we were concerned as to how to reach him. A book in our library *Dr. Bombard Goes to Sea* became his favorite. It tells of the lonely crossing of the Atlantic in a sailboat.

Charlie wanted to hear this story time and time again. The story's end may give you an idea why he liked it.

*I was going to be able to tell everyone who goes to sea what to do to stay alive on the water. But they mustn't think it's easy. If a castaway wants to live, he will have to do as I did and go through a lot of suffering and overcome great dangers, and he will have to fight against loneliness and despair all the time. He must never give up hope.*

As far as external features of books are concerned, we have to distinguish between books that we want to circulate among the children to read themselves, and books for staff and parents to read to the children. The books which the children read themselves must be easy to read (that goes for both style and print) and should be well illustrated, and they must be easy to hold while lying in bed. These points are unimportant for books to be read to the children. These should consist of brief stories, so the reading can be completed in a limited time; or else so written that the reading can be broken off and some suspense left for the next reading.

On a ward where children are in the same group for some time a story hour before nap or at bed time is good planning. The best choices for these story hours are books of real literary quality where the story and not the illustrations will keep the children's interest. Older children also enjoy books with puzzles.

Many children's magazines are available. We find the "things to do and make" pages of interest. Old catalogs entertain bed-bound children. The magazines are also a good source for current biographical sketches and scientific news items.

Junior newspapers for various age levels are helpful because they give the child a chance to read about things he hears adults mention and they have appealing pictures of current events.

## DOING USEFUL THINGS

Children eight years and up who for various reasons may have to be away from the group at times, do very well assisting a secretary or nurse in routine tasks (like stamping or sorting papers, etc.). These tasks will vary according to the ward's organization but letting children participate in some of its routine functions makes the hospital again an easier place to be in. It may not be easy to find such jobs but for some children the effort is worth while.

*Swing and slide are forgotten*
*when one can watch men at work.*

SPECIAL ACTIVITIES AND EVENTS

Besides activities that are always available, the child-care worker can plan special activities for certain days. We cook or bake about once a week.

All children enjoy popping corn. It can be popped without butter and salt, so that most children on special diets can eat it.

Little ones enjoy making simple things like applesauce and puddings.

Many suitable recipes which the older children can follow themselves can be assembled on file cards. An electric frying pan makes an excellent oven. Children of all ages are enthusiastic about icing cookies. One can buy some or bake them oneself. The children like to make cocoa, ginger bread, taffy (pulling is so much fun), pizza, doughnuts (packaged biscuits can be used if one cuts out the center). Youngsters also like to make sandwiches by cutting bread in different shapes with cookie cutters and decorating it with cream cheese colored with food coloring.

On special days, with the assistance of the dietary department, one can plan a picnic lunch and have the children prepare parts of it.

Touring the hospital in small groups interests school-age children. The kitchen and the pharmacy are most stimulating places to visit. Older children enjoy seeing the research laboratories. Newborns behind their glass wall fascinate all.

Loan exhibits can often be arranged through museums. We had unique displays from the Health Museum and a junior museum and some demonstrations from the Museum of Natural History.

We are sure that each hospital has many good ideas how to celebrate holidays and how to channel the abundance of goodwill that comes from the community through volunteers to fill the children's needs. We would like to stress the following. Have lists of gifts you want ready as early as September to give to service groups, Boy and Girl Scouts, etc., so that their efforts may be made to fit your needs. A few lists which we found helpful are in Appendix B. Through these lists we could avoid getting just stuffed animals or scrap books. A finished scrap book allows only for very passive participation from children and therefore, has only limited use.

In decorating wards for holidays, let the children plan and execute most of it. It may look less beautiful but is a lot more meaningful than to have store decorations put up. Children can draw with glass marking pencils and then paint what they outlined. Of course, the baking program will be in full swing for holidays. We like it when children can be the ones to give to family and staff rather than always being on the receiving end.

Birthdays, too, should be celebrated. There is a fine opportunity for joint planning with the child's mother.

## PLAYING OUTDOORS

In summer, some hospitals can extend the play area to the outdoors. The outside offers many outlets of aggression in acceptable ways. A child who appeared withdrawn often reacts with vigor and enthusiasm when he is outside and with familiar playground toys, away from the strange frightening atmosphere inside the hospital.

Kathy, who has a fractured femur, is being wheeled up the ramp to the playground—in her bed. She relaxes visibly in the fresh air and sunshine. Suddenly there is great excitement as a mother squirrel chases her baby. Kathy squeals with mixed fear and delight as the two race right under her bed. Her constant demands for attention are abandoned for nearly an hour as she keeps track of the squirrel family. For children on limited ambulation, such an experience takes on deep meaning.

Children who are recovering from illness or surgery or who are awaiting an operation can profit from a short play period outside. They enjoy the swing, slide, tent, wagon, rol-bac basketball, beach ball, sand, marbles, hoola hoop, pogo stick, and rubber dart game.

Certain illnesses are treated with constant parenteral medications dripping from an I.V. Tony, age ten, had septicemia, but he was feeling well. We

*Today cookies for lunch are baked.*

moved him, I.V. and all, seven floors down to the outside each day. When these expeditions started, the doctors were amazed to see him change from a whiny, uncooperative boy who was always tormenting younger children, to a boy who accepted treatments without much fuss and took new interest in getting along with the other youngsters.

Children restricted by casts, bandages or an I.V. can enjoy games from their wheel chairs or from sitting on a rubber sheet on the ground. A picnic table comes in handy. Games like Chinese checkers, dominoes, and others that can't blow away can be played outdoors. Of course all sorts of table games are played indoors as well. These children like to play card games, ring toss and rubber horse shoe tossing. They can also toss a beach ball and play with marbles and participate in stories and group singing.

# 7/Learning in the Hospital

Learning takes on a very different meaning when a child is hospitalized. Anxiety—overt or covert—is one of the unavoidable by-products of hospitalization, and so is a network of psychological defenses geared to protect the child from an unmanageable onslaught of anxiety. Such a labile state of mind is not conducive to learning. It is hard to concentrate on given or chosen tasks while preoccupied with fears about oneself.

Why then do we advocate schooling in the hospital? It is obvious why schooling is needed in long-term hospitalization. But we found it equally important for those children who stay only for a comparatively short time. Keeping up school work is of special value at the end of a term when children and their parents worry about promotion, but also for school beginners or for slow learners.

Schooling in children's hospitals is usually considered the responsibility of boards of education. Such a plan works well in chronic or convalescent hospitals which care for larger numbers of children for a considerable time. But it does not take care of the child who is only ten days on a ward, or of children in a rehabilitation unit where we believe that the teacher has to be an integral part of the clinical team, available for conferences and evaluations and in daily contact with all those who work on a child's rehabilitation.

Furthermore, there often are not enough children at a given time who are approximately on the same school level to warrant forming a class. They may also for medical reasons be unable to be in one class together. Therefore, though schooling in the hospital needs coordination with the child's home school it has to be planned individually. Still, whenever possible the stimulation which comes through working with fellow students should be utilized.

In our hospital, a child-care worker functions as the teacher; informally for those who stay only weeks rather than months, and as the tutor appointed by the child's home school for children with long hospitalization.

The teacher (child-care worker) has to be very imaginative and challenging in her teaching. She has to be inventive in her methods and has to modify her techniques continually, since she is working with a constantly changing group and with individuals whose health fluctuates from day to day. She also has to realize that for some of her children school in the past has meant disappointment, frustration, or even failure.

The following vignette shows how one of us enlisted the interest of a child who did not like school (those who do like it are no real problem).

*School evidently was a repulsive word to ten-year-old Mike, hospitalized three weeks for rheumatic fever. He wrinkled his nose and shrugged his shoulders when it was mentioned. So I said: "Why don't you come this afternoon and make a diving man?"*

*"What's a diving man?"*

*"Well, we use a little bottle inside a big bottle, and the little bottle goes up and down. It looks like magic, but there is a scientific reason why it works. I imagine you could figure it out."*

*Mike was pleased with his diver. He made good observations of what happened when the little bottle bobbed up and down and made the correct deductions as to how it worked.*

*The next day we made a crystal garden. During the measuring of materials Mike mentioned that arithmetic was his favorite subject. He asked if I could give him some numbers to divide.*

*From that day on we wheeled his bed daily to the playroom which serves as the school room for one hour each day, and Mike settled down to work.*

*Through his drawings we learned of his interest in Indians and ships and found library books which gained his attention.*

*In arithmetic we progressed from division to work with fractions, which his class was studying at the time. It was possible to introduce new steps slowly, so he could comprehend each one before advancing to new material. One day he commented: "You know, I do better in the hospital than at school."*

*He needed someone to give him constant encouragement and reassurance. The hospital school could provide this. His accomplishments there gave him the confidence that he could learn and would be able to continue with his class when he was well again.*

Letting herself be guided by Mike's interests gave this worker a chance to reach this boy. Much more complex are the questions that confront the teacher of children who have been in bed for a long time or whose bodies have changed through illness. For these children vital participation is needed to balance somewhat their enforced passivity and dependence. It is reassuring for these youngsters to find that only part of them is afflicted by the illness and that they can think as clearly as before. These children respond to teaching that makes use of their observations and thinking as well as of their fantasy.

Going to school in the hospital can be a link to the past and to the future. It reassures a child that his parents, his home school and the hospital staff all work together and believe in his getting well.

Indeed, schooling can also help recovery. A hospitalized child, who has to be passive in so many respects, should not also remain passive intellectually. Because of his limited mobility, he needs special learning tools: any child in the hospital needs concrete materials to help him integrate what he learns. Materials and the more personal contact with the teacher have to replace the stimulation that ordinarily comes through being a member of a lively group of youngsters in school.

If space and funds are available for audio-visual equipment, the education program can be greatly enriched. The use of this equipment is equally valuable for any group activity, not only for schooling.

An F.M. radio helps youngsters who are bed-bound or in isolation and is a good teaching tool for older children. They learn a lot from programs broadcast by school boards. Foreign languages, science, spelling bees, stories, and music appreciation programs are particularly liked.

A film strip projector and a few film strips are valuable equipment. Though they are often technically inferior, we prefer them to movies, as children can talk about the content of the strips as they see them. The youngsters take turns reading the captions or tell a story as they see the pictures. Many film strips are made to teach skills, others for information. Older children like to run the projector themselves. A screen is not needed as a wall or window blind works well for projecting even if the room is not very dark. Libraries have film strips for loan.

A tape recorder encourages groups of children to work together, reading

*Learning goes on in spite of chest piece and tracheotomy.*

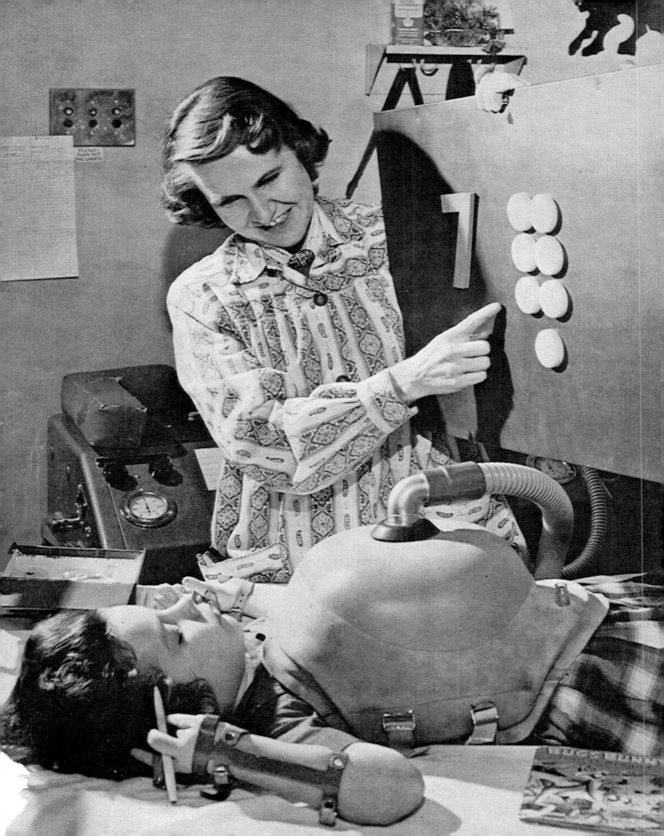

or inventing plays or recording music. Long-term patients can record letters or reports to be sent to their class at home and listen to their recorded reply. Answers to examinations can be recorded if a child can not write well.

Pictures from story books can be projected with an opaque projector to accompany a story. Children love to make their own pictures and project them while they are telling a story they have made up for it. Collections of leaves or rocks can be projected to be identified.

A movie projector is an expensive investment, and since children can participate less in films we feel it is of minor importance on a children's ward. However, an occasional movie is a real treat. Libraries or service clubs may have projectors or films for loan.

A planetarium stimulates older children. To use it during daytime needs careful darkening of the room. Telling legends about constellations and learning to identify or locate stars fascinates youngsters.

The use of television has to be somewhat regulated. It is best used on the ward where it breaks the monotony of long evenings or with children who have to wait for procedures at their bedside. It is a lifesaver for children in isolation.

Besides the aids ordinarily used for teaching reading and spelling, we found the following of great value: a felt board with attaching alphabets and numbers and number symbols; small cutout cardboard letters (capitals and small) in a box with compartments. For children with a limited range of motion this material must be small and light. Teacher-made crossword puzzles can use words from spelling lessons. A primer typewriter can be used by children or adults to type stories the children tell or to print reading material which the teacher writes for individual children.

For concept formation in arithmetic and geometry, we have used several parts of Maria Montessori's material and a magnet board.

In geography, jigsaw puzzles based on maps of the world, the United States, etc., travel games, and making relief maps, were added.

Nature study was described in the preceding chapter.

In science study, simple experiments with magnifying glass, prisms, microscope, and magnets absorb children. Some experiments which we found easy enough with careful adult preparation and assistance but still challenging enough, will be found in Appendix A.

The hospital with its many interesting departments and functions can be made a unique asset for a child's schooling. We would like to illustrate our

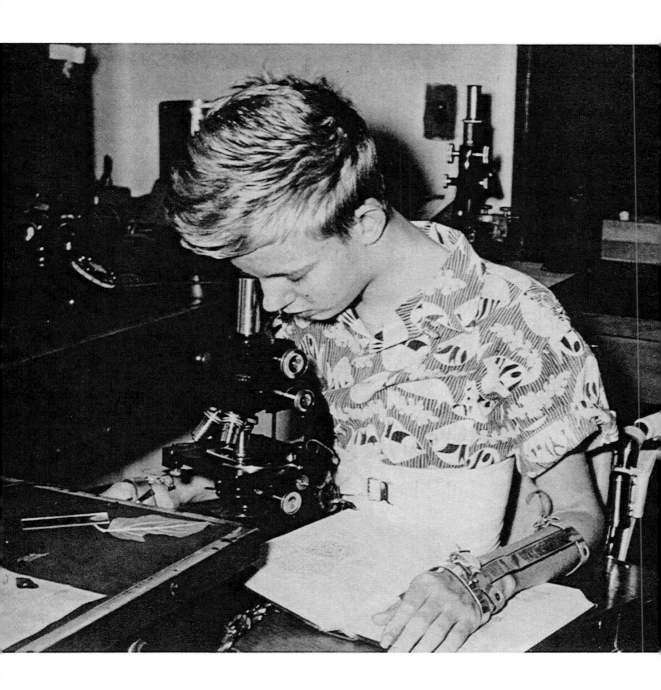

*Mark in the doctors' lab.*

point by bringing a detailed report of 16 months of tutoring of a 13-year-old boy, done by one of our workers in cooperation with the boy's home school. Though this boy was one of the last patients we saw who suffered from polio, and his experiences at first glance may not seem pertinent for today, we find the same problems in children with neurological diseases like the Werdnig-Hoffman or Guillain-Barré syndromes, or paralysis through injury of the spinal cord.

*When Mark was admitted to the Respirator Care and Rehabilitation Center, he was placed in a tank respirator. He was unable to move anything except his head. Through a mirror he could see the three or four other patients in his room. If his respirator was turned just right, he could see a tiny patch of sky and branches of a tree through a window. His mother was completely overwhelmed by the seriousness of his condition and the boy himself was passive and listless. To have something which would point to the future we started to teach Mark two weeks after the onset of his illness. As his chief interest was science, we planned to bring as much as possible of the world of science to his hospital corner.*

*Many departments of the hospital cooperated to make this possible. Plumbers and electricians collected old faucets and appliances we could disassemble. We began a collection of insects and received a pair of live praying mantes housed in a cage made by one of our carpenters. The nurses' aides and orderlies supplied a diet of flies for the mantes. When the insects died in winter, there remained a nest of eggs from which hundreds of nymphs hatched early in February.*

*The aquarium was another fascination to a boy still isolated in his corner and able to participate only by seeing and hearing. He notified us when the mother guppies were ready to deliver so they could spend their confinement in a jar of algae.*

*Other agencies facilitated our study of general science and biology as well as mathematics, English and history. The library furnished film-strips and recorded stories. The Health Museum loaned exhibits. We also utilized the radio lessons broadcast by the Cleveland Board of Education.*

*Mark prepared book reviews and reports. Since he couldn't write, we taped them. The most interesting project was a search for library material about the lac insect. He summarized this in a report and recorded it for mailing to his classmates at home.*

*His dictated letters brought pamphlets and pictures describing the city's water and sewage system, and motivated a young friend of the teacher's to visit the hospital and bring his insect collection.*

*By late spring Mark had progressed from the respirator to a rocking bed and then to a regular bed, since he needed shorter periods of respiratory help. Thus, it was easier to enlarge his world. He journeyed to our classroom by cart. When the ninth grade school year began, he could sit for short periods in a wheelchair, use his fingers supported by braces to turn pages, and slowly propel himself about with his legs which had almost recovered from the paralysis.*

*Two visits to the division's laboratory were planned, where Mark observed many diagnostic tests. Our class schedule was arranged so we could use laboratory equipment once a week. We grew bacteria from soured soup, from air, and from the aquarium water and studied them under the microscope. Yeasts, molds, protozoa from pond scum, and many common substances became more intriguing when their life processes could be studied with a microscope. The hospital supplied frogs and fish for dissection and in addition, outside the hospital building we found night crawlers, grasshoppers, and flowers for study.*

*Visits to the bacteriology laboratory and research division showed Mark vocational possibilities in the field of science and taught him more about techniques of research. The two physicians directing these divisions had prepared these visits where he met other personnel, learned more about diagnosis and treatment of diseases, and saw the elaborate equipment needed for virus research.*

*Through a staff member we learned of an enthusiastic high school science club. In order to bring young people into his hospital world, we invited them to hold meetings at our Center where Mark could join them.*

*Mark's tolerance increased. He could walk a few steps and sit three hours a day. With hands braced he could feed himself and he began the tedious process of writing. Within a few months he was ready to move home and rejoin his classmates. The day he left Cleveland for home, he stopped to accompany the science club on a tour of the Natural History Museum. When the new semester began, he resumed study in his old school starting with an hour daily. Finally he attended school full time and became an excellent student. It is gratifying to know that Mark, though still in a wheel chair, is now working on his doctorate in mathematics.*

We have described Mark's program in detail because it shows that the hospital environment itself can be a source of stimulation and exploration, and thereby counteract the isolation and depression brought about through long hospitalization.

Our notes on six-year-old Ann give quite a different picture. They also illustrate how the child acquired specific knowledge through her stay in the hospital and how a stimulating group discussion came about.

*A baby alligator was given the children for their classroom aquarium. Ann exclaimed: "Look, he frog-breathes!" ("Frog-breathing" is an auxiliary method of breathing she had learned to supplement her limited ability to breathe.) Of course, the children used the rest of that day's school session to talk about different ways of breathing—certainly an unusual topic for primary grades, but of vital interest for those whose breathing is impaired.*

*Ann was just starting to learn to read and loved to dictate stories. We typed them for her and thereby made her own reader. The story that follows shows how this child expressed feelings about her illness in her school work.*

> *I don't like cows. I am afraid of them.*
> *I don't like chickens. Just baby ones.*
> *I don't like mean boys.*
> *I don't like doctors, because they give shots.*
> *I want to give Dr. G. a shot. He don't want to have a shot, but we want to give it anyway. He is sick.*
>
> *He has to come to Cleveland.*
> *I like to give shots.*
> *I am going to tell my mother to give me a doctor's set.*
> *If I should get one, I should be very glad.*
> *I want to go home soon. I like home.*
> *I like Sue* [fellow patient] *.*

Sometimes we find children who are so overwhelmed by their sudden illness and disabilities that they put shutters on their intellectual functioning.

Peter is a good example. He became ill at the beginning of the second grade. Like so many boys, he struggled with reading and had barely started to recognize words. We became concerned, though, when Peter could not name the days of the week or tell when his birthday was. When he drew a house, he left out essential parts. He was so unresponsive that we were almost certain we had a dull child and a slow learner to work with. We asked for psychological testing. It showed that Peter had superior intelligence but an extraordinary amount of anxiety that hampered the use of his ability. We decided not to use his reader again since we had no response to the stories in it which all described the carefree things children do, all very remote and out of reach for a child who is immobilized and fifty miles away from home. Therefore, we decided to make our own reading material. We wrote him little notes on things he might be thinking of and passed them to him in a secretive way, like "your mother will be here to see you tomorrow" or "we will ask Dr. Green to bring the puppy again from the Lab to visit you" or similar things. Thereby, we established the idea of reading as a means of communication.

The breakthrough came when his teacher showed him, on a large globe, the route of a long and interesting journey she had taken some years ago. Then we saw the child really light up with interest and participation, reading with excitement words like Pacific Ocean, Hawaii, etc. When I came into his classroom that day, he called excitedly, "Mrs. Plank, put the world on my stomach, I want to show you where Japan is." From then on we had no more trouble to interest Peter in learning. What helped him to use his intelligence freely again was probably a combination of his strengthened relationship to his teacher and her skill in giving him unusual materials.

We have observed in several children that the anxiety which was mobilized through severe illness made these youngsters more receptive to learning than they had been before they were in the hospital. This gain in interest and in the quality of learning was retained after their return home.

# 8/Children Tell Stories and Draw

Another stimulation for learning comes through creative writing. When we listen to the stories children tell and look carefully at the pictures they draw, we learn a lot about what illness means to them. Creativity, certainly, is curbed by the anxiety connected with hospitalization, and in our sample also by the limited experience with graphic art, typical of our population, who mostly grow up in poverty areas. The children's language and thoughts, though, are spontaneous and most vivid in their directness. Few write their stories; most children dictate them. Regardless, they come through charmingly.

Here is Tommy, a hemophiliac and slow learner with a delightful sense of humor in his fantasies:

*THE HOSPITAL*
*I like nurses and the doctors and four of the playladies. I like toys in the hospital—anyones—the cars and the horse and the puzzles. I like them the favorite.*

*I don't like my I.V. and I want to get out of bed 'cause I hate to stay in bed. Do you want to take my place and get in bed for me? Then I'd be the playlady.*

*WHEN I GET HOME*
*We moved, so I'm gonna go to that playground that I don't know very good, but I'm gonna go anyway. I'm gonna go on the top of the hill and roll all the way down and break my neck, and I'll be back in the hospital with my breaked neck!*

58

*ABOUT HORSES*
*I made the children horses fight their mother. I made the baby horse kick his mother in the rear end. She beats them up—but they're flying horses and fly away.*

Compare Tommy's fantasies with the most realistic description of Gary, another hemophiliac, a year older and well cared for by a mother who, like Tommy's mother, is on Aid to Dependent Children:

*MY VISITS TO THE HOSPITAL*
*I have been to the hospital thirty-seven times to date. The first time I was in the hospital was four days before my first birthday. Since I was so little I can't remember most of my hospital visits in the past. I do know that I bit my tongue seven times, and the first time I went to the hospital. But the next six times my mother treated me at home. A lot of times when I've been bleeding from my mouth while losing my baby teeth, there would be blood all over the pillow case and the whole bed. If a person walked into the house, they would think that someone had been murdered there! I have a bed sore on the back of my head from the first time I was in the hospital. That was because they put a transfusion through a vein in my head and I had to lay in that one position for over a week with sandbags around my head.*

*They diagnosed my case of hemophilia a little quicker because they had had another case of hemophilia and have spent over twenty-four hours trying to diagnose his disease. His name was Ken. He came in when he was nine months old. So all they had to do was to compare my blood with his and they diagnosed my case in about six hours. The doctors said my mother would have to get a harness for me but my mom never did like harnesses because she felt that little boys and girls should not be strapped down that way—like on a leash.*

*Hemophilia is inherited from the female side of the family. Unless the male has hemophilia and he marries a carrier, the girls cannot get hemophilia. Records are proving that the Kings and Queens of Spain and other European countries had male hemophiliacs. People are claiming that the son of the Czar of Russia had hemophilia and his legs were so swollen that they were all twisted and folded.*

*When I was two and one-half, we were downstairs in the living room of our landlady. There were two girls, five and three years old. We were jumping in turns on a big panda bear when all of a sudden she thought that it was her turn and I thought it was my turn, so I jumped—and she jumped right on top of me! And she twisted my left arm. During the night I was moaning in pain, and my arm was gradually stiffening up, so the next morning it was all doubled up into a fist. My mother took me to the hospital and they put a cast on it. Right now I am ten and seven-twelfths years old, and my fingers and wrist still aren't completely loosened.*

*Most likely I have a lot more hospital visits ahead of me, but if they discover a cure soon enough, I might just have a few more hospital visits ahead of me. When I grow up, if I get there, I plan to discover a cure for hemophilia—if someone doesn't beat me to it. My other goal in life is to invent an anti-gravity belt, or a serum that you can drink to have that power. A lot of people think that this is a silly idea, but I really mean it. People in 1900 laughed at the Wright brothers, and in the future the people of 2000 will laugh at me. But I really mean it.*

*God gave me hemophilia for a special reason: and that reason is He probably wanted me to perfect a cure for hemophilia. In a way I'm not sorry I have hemophilia—but it's given me great experiences that I might need to know in the future.*

Eleven-year-old Dora was in the hospital for nine months for multiple orthopedic problems. She did very poorly in school before her hospitalization:

*It's Saturday morning. First I wake up. Then I wash up. Then I put on my clothes; go down the stairs; look in the refrigerator; find something to eat.*

*When I finish, I clean up the house: clean the kitchen up; go upstairs, clean upstairs; come back downstairs, play the record player, dance and sing. I do the "4 Corners," "The Horse," "Hand Dance," and "The Pimp." Two records I like are "I'm Going To Make You Love Me" by the Temptations and the Supremes, and "Heard It Through the Grapevine."*

*When I finished, I wait for Momma. She's been shoppin'. Then I sit down and play with my nieces. I have 3 nieces. All girls, no boys. I pick and clean up again ('cause of my 2 nieces). When they leave, I get to the record player. I finish playin' the record player, I sit down and talk to my sisters, my Momma, and my brother. We go eat. My favorite lunch is boiled ham and ice cold Pepsi, and my favorite dessert is ice cream.*

*Now I shall close this letter with a kiss to Momma. I love you Momma.*

This certainly is primitive writing, but the child's sincerity and eagerness give it a warm and eloquent quality.

Lester, age eleven, suffered from sickle cell anemia:

*I was in my house sitting.*
*And people were hollering.*
*Car horns were blowing out on the street.*
*Cats were meowing inside.*
*Kids tiptoe to hide.*
*There was a gang meeting out on the street.*
*Then the telephone rang.*
*The pots started to bang.*
*They were picking up the cans out on the street.*
*I could not stand the noise out on the street.*

Diane, age ten, wrote her story herself:

*ABOUT MY SUGAR DIABETES*
*I get mad if I see chocolate cake or something like that because that's my favorite, chocolate cake and fudge. I can't eat it because I have sugar diabetes. So, it makes me mad because if I would eat it I'd wind up in the hospital. I'd be in the hospital if I would eat it because sugar goes against my insulin. In some way it works through my kidneys, gets in my urine, and my urine shows I have sugar. When I have sugar in my urine, it shows that I have lots of sugar in my body and it proves that I have sugar diabetes. Having too much sugar in my body makes me have dizzy spells, throw up a lot, and I feel drowsy and want to sleep all the time. When I'm in a coma, I lay and whine all the time, my mouth is dry, and when I drink something, I throw it back up. Then I lay down and go to sleep. When I wake up, I'm in the hospital.*
*Those shots. They ain't very pleasant but I take them.*

Norma, age thirteen, hospitalized with severe burns, wrote the following letter:

*Dear Judy:*

*How are you? I am not fine. It's a long story so have plenty of time to read this. I am writing this in the hospital a few days before I will go home. Well, I've been here for seven weeks. I'll tell you in number form. No.1 My house burned down! No.2 I almost died! No.3 They saved my life! (the hospital)  No.4 Now I am all healed almost! No.5 That's why I haven't written to you! No.6 It happened two days before Christmas. No.7 It happened the night I typed a letter to you! It never got mailed! Just burned! Well, anyhow, please don't cry! It was all very horrible! Boo Hoo. I will send you the newspaper clippings. Thank you for your Christmas card. I spent Christmas, New Years, and my birthday here. It will be good to get home now. Here's what happened!*

*Fire Escape*

*Anyhow it was Dec. 22. I just finished typing to you. I went to bed. About 1:30 at night I woke up. I smelled smoke. Fire, I yelled! I woke up my family! We all ran out on the upstairs back porch. We yelled for help! None came!! I was choking and crying and yelling help! My ma let go of me and I ran back in the fire, but I don't remember it. Then I woke up in a hospital yelling for water. I got* none!

Self-expression through writing helps children retain or regain their self-image and give us insight into their thoughts and feelings. Let's now turn to another medium, namely graphic expression. The drawings and painting show how children interpret the threats of illness and let us in on their thoughts.

Seven-year-old Nancy suffered from rheumatic fever complicated by severe pericarditis. She was very irritable, unusually fearful of x-rays and blood drawings.

After a stormy visit to x-ray, we asked her whether she would like to draw what was done there. Nancy eagerly produced the following drawing (Fig. 1). The x-ray table is clearly visible with the heart on it. I asked what was around the heart and Nancy indignantly answered: "Don't you see, these are the murmurs. If a murmur touches my heart I must die." No wonder she put up such a fight about going to x-ray! This teaches us still another lesson: Nancy had picked up the word *murmurs* on rounds—and since many medical students were asked to listen to her murmurs, they took a threatening form in the child's fantasy. This drawing allowed us to talk to

*Figure 1*

Nancy about her fears and to explain to her that murmurs can only be heard, but have no shape. A previous talk about the organ system of the human body also was absorbed and reproduced: the little girl in the picture shows the heart and G.I. tract under her dress. We certainly could not change Nancy's personality structure which had marked hysterical components, but by dealing with her open questions and worries, we could help her to a speedy recovery and a much easier time at the hospital.

The drawings of Louis helped us in establishing our relationship with him. He is a brain-damaged inner-city child, one of eleven children, who is suffering from Christmas disease, a hemophilia-like illness. Since he had serious intracranial bleeding as a very young child, his vision is gone in one eye. The highest I.Q. he ever achieved in testing was 56. Communicating through language was exceedingly difficult. But this child told us in his drawings what he could not put into sentences. His attention to details is astounding. Louis was not in school until he was ten years old and we could find a place for him in a newly opened class for retarded, physically handicapped children. Two of his innumerable drawings are reproduced here (Figs. 2 and 3).

The dinosaur is a touching wish fulfillment. Though he has swollen knees (they look like Louis' when he's bleeding into his knee joints), he is on roller skates, an impossibility for a bleeder who wears a long leg brace and has poor vision. The other drawing transmits the feelings of misery Louis experiences at admission during a bleeding episode.

*Figure 2*

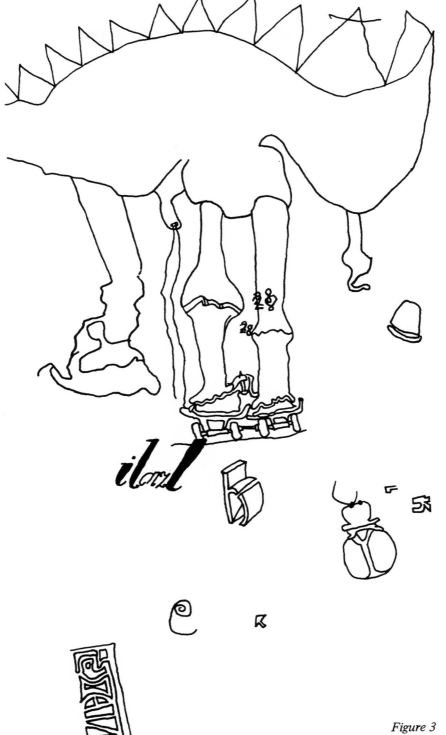

Figure 3

Our next pictures (Figs. 4-6) are a series of three. A very intelligent eleven-year-old boy who had to undergo liver surgery, drew them. They don't need my comments. They tell their story directly.

*Figure 4*

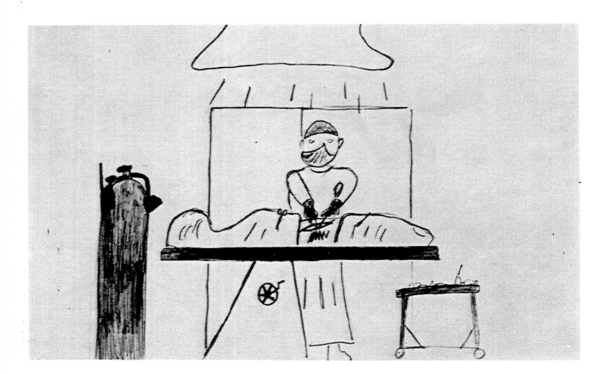

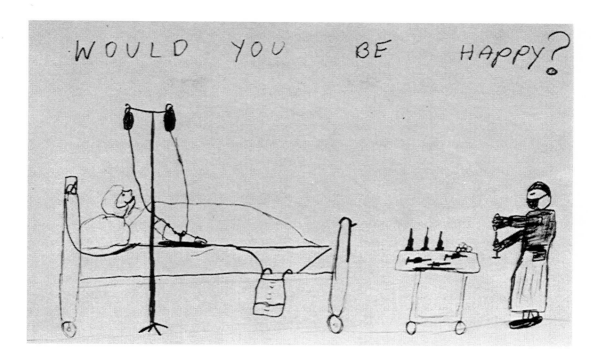

*Figure 5*

*Figure 6*

The last, a painting (Fig. 7) done by a fourteen-year-old boy, expresses the misery an adolescent finds himself in when hospitalized. These feelings are accentuated when procedures have be done in the genital area. This boy suffered from unexplained hematuria. He painted the picture and dictated the poem reproduced under the painting to accompany it:

*A Walk Into Nothingness*

*It's just mostly like the end of the world.*
*With broken down buildings and torn up land*
*And you're the only one left*
*And you're all alone*
*Walking into nothingness.*

This could be any adolescent's feelings about himself—but there was an additional quality of hopelessness which made me look at the picture again. The boy had no hands! Our observations were shared with his student doctor. Jointly we worked out a plan how he could discuss the problems of puberty, particularly masturbation, with the boy. Since none of the tests brought any evidence of disease, they were stopped. The boy, greatly relieved by his frequent talks with his doctor, returned to his fatherless home, strengthened by his hospitalization.

These observations could only be made because the environment of the activity rooms allowed for this freedom of expression.

Figure 7

# 9/A Child Life
## and Education Program

In the preceding chapters of this book, we have reviewed the problems that hospitalization of children entails and various approaches to solving them. To sum up our experiences by way of presenting a comprehensive example, we here describe the Child Life and Education Program (as we call it) as it actually developed in our hospital.

The whole clinical team, of which the child-care worker is a member, decides on the living patterns of the children on the different wards. The child-care worker, though, has the function of implementing such plans. I cannot stress strongly enough how much good child care depends on a team that works spontaneously and passes information quickly and informally between disciplines in a continuous flow rather than waiting for formal conferences and consultations.

In the description of our different services, we shall put emphasis on those experiences that have a more general validity and that may be applicable to other medical problems and in other hospitals. We may draw occasionally on previous experiences with illnesses that hardly occur anymore (like poliomyelitis), but the principles and methods we used are applicable for children with other diseases.

THE PEDIATRIC OUT-PATIENT CLINIC

Our main object in the clinic is to get children to settle down while they are waiting for medical attention and to relieve their boredom and anxiety. But our work in the clinic also offers an opportunity for observations which can give the doctor clues for the diagnosis or the assessment of the educability of a child.

We organized a spacious waiting room by dividing it into two areas: one for adults and those children who want to stay with them, the other for children at play. Movable shelves with books or toys on both sides form the partition. An aquarium, centrally located, attracts many children. Film strips or slides are shown occasionally; these can also be used for parent education. As an extra treat for the children a traveling zoo comes once a month for a visit.

Materials for play have to be well organized and quickly available, since some children spend little time in the waiting area. Group activities, too, are rather limited, as children have to go to the examining room as soon as they are called. Noise would add confusion, so fairly quiet activities must be planned.

There is no need for a child in a clinic to establish a strong relationship with one worker; it is all right if the child finds a different person each time he comes to clinic as long as the direction stays in the hands of one competent person. The clinic may therefore be staffed by one professional worker and volunteers. We have an interesting arrangement whereby four high school seniors work four hours each day and get credit as this work is part of a training program in child care.

The volunteer, child-care worker, or nurse can plan many structured activities such as reading or telling stories (using a flannel board for illustration), record playing, singing, or finger plays. Decorating the play area for different seasons or holidays with the children is a fine project.

The following pieces of equipment and materials were found useful in our clinic: for infants and toddlers, a foam rubber mat on the floor, rocking toys, a small, non-rocking wooden box to sit in, balls that don't bounce, and a limited number of push-and-pull toys that are not noisy; for older children, tables and chairs of varied size and height, books and magazines, crayons and paper or coloring sheets (cut-up coloring books), peg boards, puppets and stuffed animals. An FM radio can provide a pleasant background sound for both parents and children.

If a worker is available to supervise the play area continuously, puzzles, table games, and other toys which have many small parts are good. If there is no supervision, too many pieces get lost and the games lose their value. Plastic bricks, construction sets, a doll house and dolls, wooden beads or spools to string, plants to water, and fish to feed attract many children. A stethoscope, a syringe, and nurses' caps offer opportunities for dramatic play.

In the examining rooms, we have made a few simple arrangements so that children will be less frightened. To avoid the unease of being lifted up onto an examining table, we have provided steps so that the child can climb onto the table himself. We have mobiles which the child can easily see while on his back. He may enjoy handling a simple toy as he waits while the doctor talks with his parent; we suggest rather large toys, since these are more likely to stay in the examining room than smaller ones.

## THE GENERAL PEDIATRIC DIVISION

Two wards of twenty-four beds each comprise this division. One ward serves infants and toddlers up to the age of two and a half years. Ages in the other ward go up from two and a half practically through the teens. Everything but contagious disease is cared for on this division.

We started by setting up one room on this floor as a playroom with equipment that would allow children of varied ages to be active and to become absorbed. From this one room we branched out into three rooms and created an outdoor summer play area. Since there is enough space now, we can include children from ten months and older in the Child Life Program.

The three rooms are staffed from 9:00 to 5:00 with a child-care worker, two students from a college that operates under a work-study plan, and a nursing student. The college students work for three months on the "service." The nursing student comes for a limited assignment during her pediatric experience.

The cooperation of these workers, one fully trained and mature, the others young but carefully selected for personality and motivation, offers what we think hospitalized children need: continuity in contact, knowledge about the condition of children in hospitals, vigor and enthusiasm. But most important is their sensitivity to the often unexpressed needs of children under stress—their ability to reach out, to make children feel secure and wanted in their presence, is essential.

On a ward of this kind, and especially in a teaching hospital, one may come into contact with children whose illness or past history requires delicate understanding in handling and constant coordination of effort that cannot be achieved with a changing group of volunteers. Still, the volunteer remains important for special purposes. It is nice to have entertainments during holidays or at regular intervals, such as a weekly movie or puppet plays, given by a volunteer service. But a healthy child's day is not built around entertainment, and a sick child's should be even less. Children do not need diversion to get well, but rather opportunities to participate with all available emotional and intellectual energy in daily living.

The playroom and its personnel have to prepare a setting to meet these needs. Therefore, on a general pediatric ward the goals of a child life and education program can be summarized as follows:

*1. To provide a setting for children of all ages where they can find play and activities that interest and absorb them, counteract their loneliness and anxiety, and help to turn the passivity of the patient into the activity of the growing child.*

*2. To give children a chance to interact with others away from their cubicle, to form relationships to adults as well as to other children, to help them work through the basic fears inherent in illness and hospitalization, to reassure them about or prepare them for procedures and surgery.*

*3. To help school-age children to continue with some of their school work while hospitalized.*

*4. To arrange specific opportunities for play under direction of a skilled worker where fantasies or traumatic experience in relation to hospitalization can be played out and worked through.*

*5. To provide an area where parents can visit and play with their child as part of an ongoing program. At the time when parents have to leave, the child finds himself with others and can be more easily reassured.*

*6. To help children at mealtimes to accept hospital food or limiting diets, by providing good groupings at mealtimes with a chance for conversation and informality.*

## LONG-TERM HOSPITALIZATION

On an acute ward, with the daily changes of patients and their medical management, long-term hospitalization for either rehabilitation or convalescent treatment brings out additional problems for the child-care worker. Special considerations have to be given to these long-term patients. There are different reasons for the long stay:

1. Illnesses that need constant and highly specialized medical and nursing care, e.g., children who are in daily need of artificial respiration and special feedings. (I am thinking of progressive neurological disorders or of those illnesses that improve slowly like the Guillain-Barré Syndrome.)

2. Children suffering from tuberculosis who, after being worked up and responding to chemotherapy, could go home if their families could only receive them. For the latter patients the child-care worker has to counteract many potentially damaging factors, particularly the separation from home and the frequent difficulty in planning with the parents for the child's needs. We try to arrange for parents to visit even if they themselves are hospitalized. One mother, who was hospitalized for tuberculosis in another division of our hospital, came daily to play for an hour with her two little sons; this helped her medical progress as well as the boys' adjustment. Another mother, a patient in a different hospital, called her four-year-old regularly once a day on the telephone. Casework services which help parents find their role with their hospitalized child thereby help the child indirectly.

3. Another special group of patients are the failures to thrive and the battered children. They, too, stay longer than we would wish, since a sound plan for their future lives has to be worked out first to prevent a potentially dangerous repetition of neglect or abuse. The observations on the battered child's interaction and ability to play will assist in planning for him, even when the actual plans must be settled by court action.

When there is no longer a serious medical problem these children's needs become very decidedly the child-care worker's concern. She has to help them to cope with the separation from their families without losing the feeling of belonging to and being wanted by them. She also has to provide the emotional and intellectual stimulation, often long delayed, which is necessary for healthy development. The ward has to feel like a home within the hospital. The playroom and the outdoor play yard are set up with those goals in mind. They are equipped for all activities children enjoy: block building and dramatic play, painting and modeling, play with water and sand. Climbing, sliding, and swinging, as well as music activities, have their place. In a little housekeeping corner children can do some actual cooking and baking. Outdoors, winding paved paths provide space for wagons and tricycles, grassy nooks for quiet play. As mentioned in Chapter 7, we also continue schooling as a vital part of the older child's day.

Many activities are planned to counteract the sterility of hospital living. The children eat in small groups, resembling family units. Pets are brought in for several weeks at a time, through the help of volunteers from a junior museum. Where possible, children wear their own clothes, but often clothes have to be provided through gifts from volunteers and service groups.

Though staffing conditions in a general hospital do not allow one woman to assume the mother role for these children at all times, it seems that the dedication of the charge nurse and the child-care worker can to a large degree make up for this serious deficiency.

One aspect of hospital living that concerns us during prolonged stays is the lack of men in the children's lives. The only men most children encounter are the physicians, and as these often rotate through the services, their contacts may be brief and irregular. Therefore, we make a conscious effort to have thoughtful and kindly men around in the daily non-professional services of a ward. The gardener or maintenance man often becomes an object for friendship and identification for the children. At times we have succeeded in bringing a graduate student to participate regularly for a semester in the children's play program.

A special situation arises if the sick child has no family contact while he is hospitalized. A wide variety of reasons may account for this: illness in a one-parent family; confinement of a parent in a mental hospital; the necessity of sending the child for treatment to a large medical center far from home. I was particularly impressed with the needs of children from Public Health Service Indian Hospitals, where the inability to communicate in English aggravated the situation; or with those of Eskimo children whom I saw or heard about who were sent as far as Rochester, Minnesota—or Rochester, New York—for special surgery.

All these children need our most careful planning. Let me describe a situation where no social pathology or other family disruptions influenced the lack of visiting and what we did about it:

*In one of the harshest winters of the last decade, a fifteen-months-old boy was sent to our hospital from a remote Pennsylvania farm. This little boy's legs got gangrenous after chicken-pox. Amputation had to be considered, and was finally performed. Both the distance and the terrible winter weather made it impossible for the parents to come more often than every other weekend. Of course our little patient could not yet communicate through language, and to make things worse, a board had to be fastened to his stumps to correct contractures. Therefore, he could only lie in bed or be held; he could not sit. We decided to assign one of the workers from the playroom permanently to him; she was to be with him for most of his waking hours. Our student worker, a most mature and sensitive person, could bring him to the playroom or spend time with him alone and find activities that were satisfying for one who had to be flat in bed; but most importantly, she was his. During the two months of their contact she could help him somewhat to express his needs and wishes, partially through words. The worker had to learn that though she gave of herself like a mother, she would have, without regret, to relinquish him to his real mother after a while. She had to make a delicate adjustment in order to provide for him without expecting the return gratification of seeing the final results of her great efforts: to see him walk again. A year and a half after his discharge we could send her the photograph of a smiling boy walking on his two prostheses.*

Children with prolonged hospitalization often find that the family constellation changes while they are away from home. Families move, new babies are born, and a parent may have left the home because of illness or other reasons. It is almost trite to mention that if a new baby arrives while the child is hospitalized, it must seem to him like a substitute for him, since he is "no good any more." This experience confronted us vividly with little Johnny.

Three-year-old Johnny was waiting to be placed in a foster home. After an interval of months, his mother, a shiftless and promiscuous woman, came unannounced for a visit and took Johnny home for the day. He was overjoyed to see his older sister, but was confronted with a new-born baby girl for the first time, though he had been told about her. Upon his return to the hospital, he was sad and listless, and in an almost panicky way insisted that he be dressed in girls' clothing, including girls' shoes. It was obvious that this was not a playful whim but had some deeper meaning. When the same thing happened the next day, we told him that we had lots of dress-up clothes he could use if he wanted to pretend that he was a little girl, but that he was Johnny, a little boy, and that we liked him and knew his mother liked little boys, too. He could choose his shirt and pants, but we would not dress him as a girl.

Poor Johnny—though he could not depend on his mother at all and had seen her only once or twice during his long hospital stay, he was so gripped by his visit home that he felt if only he were a girl his mother would take him home to stay. Only after his favorite child-care worker had assured him that she liked little boys and liked Johnny particularly, could he give up pretending to be a girl and slowly resume his identity.

The emotional impact of an illness which brings conditions that cannot be cured, but only ameliorated through rehabilitation treatment, sets a very different climate for the child-care worker. A mature and experienced worker is essential. She will need maturity and patience to tolerate the emotional demands such children make on those who work with them, and she also has to accept unexpected breaking-through of hostility. We do not assign college students to them.

Children who undergo serious body changes and are severely restrained in their motility through illness develop a distorted image of their body and its functions. Since they are unable to carry out independently such functions as eating or elimination, they at times are thrown back into feelings of a much younger child. We find it very important to use all available substitutes, meager as they may be, to allow these children to function on their proper developmental level. Food is served family style and the children have some choice. They may visit the hospital kitchen or have some foods prepared on their ward, or are taken out for picnics. They are encouraged to assist in their bath, particularly to wash their own genitals. A mirror is hung in the tub room so that those children who are completely paralyzed and have no way to see or feel their body shape can, without having to ask and to believe others, see for themselves that the damage done to muscle functioning does not distort the rest of their body.

Play becomes very important and often taxes the imagination and patience of those who try to provide it. The playroom is almost the only place, other than meals, where these children can make choices.

Schooling plays a very vital part in their rehabilitation. In our chapter on learning in the hospital, we have discussed this question in great detail.

## THE CONTAGIOUS DISEASE DIVISION

We have one child-care worked assigned to "contagion." She is responsible for children in isolation as well as for those who, after chemotherapy, are considered non-contagious and can be on an open ward and in the play area.

This unit is of course a most dramatic one, with constant arrivals and departures of critically ill patients and with unexpected emergencies arising. Let me describe one such emergency:

*Infectious hepatitis brought five little boys, ages seven to ten, from a home for dependent children to the hospital. These boys presented a classic emergency on the isolation ward. After a few days they felt quite well again, but their illness required continued isolation and bed rest. Visiting is permitted in this ward, but their families, for reasons that brought these children into a receiving home in the first place, were available only in a most limited way to visit the children.*

*The nurses on that service usually deal with infants or with severely ill patients in private rooms. Therefore, they excel in nursing skills and devotion to patients but have no experience with groups of children who feel comparatively well. To add to the problems of management, these boys functioned like an impenetrable closed society: they had known each other for months from living together in the children's home. The child-care staff was called in for special staffing after a succession of destructive acts one night, which not only were intolerable but endangered the children themselves.*

*We quickly had to shift gears. Instead of our usual encouragement and permissiveness, we had to let these boys know that we would control them. The children had to know that we would follow all medical restrictions, regardless of their wishes to the contrary. They had to feel how much we cared for them and that we would try to make things interesting and pleasant, but that we would be able to control their hostility and destructiveness. We had to assess how to equip this ward, which materials could be used as a release of tensions, without being too stimulating for our little gang of boys.*

*We had to reassign our own time immediately to free one of us so that she could spend as much time as possible with these youngsters. The two most experienced workers divided their time on this ward and received additional help from a member of the   hospital's social service staff, who came for an hour daily.*

Someone in the hospital has to be available to be "the child's advocate." Physicians and nurses often fulfill this mission; they have the duty, and the skill, to recognize special needs of children. Especially in smaller hospitals which cannot afford an elaborate separate child life and education program, the children can still get the essential benefits if nurses take over this function. In larger hospitals, however, the other responsibilities of nurses and doctors are so pressing that they rarely have the time to stay with a child or to work with a group of children. The child-care worker, as a member of the clinical team, can do just that.

It will have become clear to the reader that child-care workers need a sound core of knowledge about children. They have to know how children normally behave at a given age and in different cultural groups, but they also have to understand how the many facets of illness and hospital experience may modify this normal behavior. They have to learn about the dynamics of child development.

A great deal of learning goes on during the weekly in-service training, when workers can present some of the problems they face with children and then discuss, within their group, ways of overcoming them.

Throughout the years the workers in our program have come from different fields: nursery education, special education, nursing, child welfare, psychology, child development, and even from medicine. They could also be recruited from social group work, occupational or recreational therapy.

The child-care worker focuses on the child as such rather than on the child's sickness, but she has to understand the illness, the child's reaction to it, and the defenses the child uses to cope with his reactions. She has to understand especially how anxiety or denial may affect a child's functioning and what she can do to help prevent or undo emotional damage. She works with the strength in the child's ego, and she has to learn to recognize and develop it so that she can help him in dealing with life in the hospital.

# *Appendixes*

## A. CRAFTS AND EXPERIMENTS

It is not our purpose to provide a manual of arts and crafts. We assume that the reader who wants to do such work is familiar with the methods or can learn about them from other sources. We are merely giving lists of activities that we have found especially useful for hospitalized children, with brief hints on how to do them.

*Painting and Drawing.* Painting on newsprint attached to an easel is a favorite. Rigatoni (large macaroni) can be painted and strung, making necklaces. Make puppets by painting faces and clothes on tongue blades, then tape a string to the back. Spatter-painting through window screen attached to a wooden frame, and making ink blots is fun. Finger painting with powdered finger paint, liquid paint in starch, or powdered paint in liquid soap is a good outlet for the active child. Use a table top, tray or slick paper (shelf paper) for finger painting. Stimulate interest in drawing with different drawing materials such as charcoal, colored chalk on construction paper and wax crayons on canvas. (Iron the canvas after coloring to dye the cloth.)

*Cutting and Pasting.* Use scraps of colored paper, and various textured cloth to make collages. Make mobiles using thin sticks, free forms from colored paper or nature objects. (Start with the bottom of the mobile and work toward the top.) Children design hats of newspapers or of paper plates using yarn, crepe paper and Kleenex for decorations. Papier maché will dry over night if a little starch paste is added to bits of paper; thin coats of this

*80*

mixture are applied to balloons to make globes and heads, or to a greased saucer to make a plate.

*Weaving, Braiding, Stringing, and Lacing.* Gimp is useful for lacing leather articles. Shoe factories often donate soft leather, or scraps can be purchased at craft shops. Children design comb cases, purses and so forth on cardboard, then trace them onto the leather. For this craft, you will also need scissors, a leather punch, snap setter, snaps and a hammer. Twisted crepe paper (an inexpensive twister can be purchased) can be woven around a heavy paper cup with slits from top to bottom around the side. (Cut an odd number of slits.) Shellac the product or spray it with plastic. Strips of construction paper or folded newspaper can be woven into mats. Make holders by punching holes around a paper plate and half of another plate and lacing them together with heavy yarn. Weaving pot holders or mats on looms is popular. Older children can make cane baskets. Dye plastic intravenous tubing with Rit, cut it into pieces, and string necklaces or bracelets. The very young like to string painted spools.

*Molding and Carving.*    Children never tire of making plaster of paris figures. Rubber molds cost a few cents at craft shops, and hospitals have plaster of paris. Mix two parts plaster with about one part lukewarm water and pour the mixture quickly into inverted molds. Setting time takes about thirty minutes. (In cleaning up, avoid clogging drains with scraps of plaster.) Ceramic clay interests all ages. Children also like to make play dough to pound or form. Use two parts flour, one part salt, a little tempera for color and just enough water to hold it together. Store it in tight containers. Papier mache makes a strong puppet head. As base, make a cardboard tube about three inches high and large enough to fit over three fingers. Form the mixture around the top two inches of the tube, shaping a head. When the head is dry (one or two days) paint and shellac it, then staple a cloth skirt to the tube below the head. Carving soap interests children. Use plastic knives. Cut raised designs on a white potato, brush paint on the design, and use this to stamp prints on paper.

*Sewing and Using Yarn.* Girls and little boys, too, enjoy sewing. Felt is a good material for beginners. While hospitalized, older girls like to baste skirts for themselves for someone at home to sew on the machine. Older girls draw on muslin and embroider the design. Yarn can be used to make dolls and flowers. Girls enjoy learning to knit or crochet with heavy cotton yarn and quickly make belts, hair bands and pot holders.

*Woodwork*. You need a carpenter's horse, hammer, coping saw, vise, nails with broad heads, sandpaper and scraps of soft wood. The three-and-four-year olds pound nail after nail into the wood, while older children make boxes, airplanes, cars, doll furniture, and many unnameable articles.

*Science Projects*. Solar system mobile: paint the milky way on a long oval cardboard and paint cardboard discs to represent the sun and planets. Suspend the milky way from a lamp or the ceiling.

Youngsters learn how crystals form by making a *crystal garden*. Mix two tablespoons each of water, salt and bluing with one-half teaspoon of ammonia. Pour this over lumps of coal in a pie pan. To color the crystals, use a few drops of liquid paint. In a few hours, formations of crystals appear on the coal.

*"Magic Diving Man."* This experiment demonstrates that air occupies space. You need: a quart glass jar, a small bottle which easily slips into the jar, rubber from an inner tube or heavy balloon to cover the quart jar, string, a glass marking pencil, and water. Draw a man on the small bottle, then fill it about ¾ full of water. Fill the quart jar completely with water, then invert the small bottle quickly into the jar so that little of the water in the bottle is spilled. If the bottle floats, tap it gently to see if it will go to the bottom and return. If it doesn't, try a different amount of water in the little bottle until it does respond to a gentle tap. Then pour about one inch of water out of the quart jar. Cover the jar with the rubber stretched tightly over it and tie the rubber around the neck of the jar with the string. Now press on the rubber and the bottle will sink to the bottom of the jar. Release the rubber and the bottle will float. Children soon observe the change in water level in the little bottle and discover why the magic man dives.

*Blueprinting* is used to make interesting designs. Store the paper in a tightly covered roll in a dark place. When you are about to use it, unwrap the paper and cut in into sheets. Have the children place objects or lay their heads on the sheets in the sunlight. If the sunlight is bright, within five minutes the exposed areas will fade. Dip the sheets into a mixture of about half hydrogen peroxide and half water and spread the sheets on a flat surface to dry. A deep blue profile of the objects is the final result.

## B. EQUIPMENT AND SUPPLIES

*Equipment.* Basic equipment for play and learning activities will have to be purchased. In our hospital permanent equipment was bought with donations from different groups in the community. Our budget for supplies, too, comes from service clubs. However, the good will and generosity of such groups needs the direction of the professional worker to select the right things.

In buying furniture watch for weight, as tables and chairs have to be moved constantly. Consider the height of wheel chairs and have at least one table under which they fit. The right height of tables and chairs is important. Round or half round tables are particularly good for very young children. A choice of practical as well as good looking children's furniture is available from child equipment firms, but not in department stores or hospital supply houses. Different pieces of equipment (like easels or small tables) can be constructed by the hospital or by volunteers. Donated cut-outs from sink counters make excellent formica tops. Don't forget to have some wash basins mounted low and one small toilet for the use of the younger children.

*Supplies.* Many supplies are available in most hospitals from various departments, such as Central Supply, Kitchen, Carpentry Shop. Nurses and physicians often have discarded equipment for playroom use. Thoughtful individuals, scout troops, and clubs will ask what they may provide. Here are some suggestions of things to collect:

Embroidery floss and yarn
Felt (as old hats, washed)
Scraps of material for doll
    dresses, etc.
Books and records
Dress-up clothes (as man's vest,
    hat, belt, jewelry, and purses)

Crayons and pencils
Coloring books and punch-out
    books
Rubber dolls and used toys
    in good condition
Containers and cigar boxes
Plants

Small amounts of money will buy playing cards, balloons, and models to assemble.

*Useful Kits Which Can Be Assembled:*

1. Cut and paste kit: blunt scissors, jar of paste, brush, assorted shapes and sizes of colored paper and sheets of plain paper.

2. Paint kit: eight assorted colors of water paint, plain paper, water pan and brush (¼ inch).

3. Magnet kit: small magnet with string attached, collection of metal, wooden and cloth items, small pictures on cardboard with staples.

4. Wood construction kit: small assorted blocks of soft wood, nails, small hammer, sand paper, wheels, small jars of oil base paint, turpentine and a brush.

5. Carving kit: large bars of soft soap with plastic knife and pictures of animals, boats and statues for ideas.

6. Wood gluing kit: ice cream sticks, wood glue, rubber bands.

7. Sewing kit: small doll (6" or 8"), scissors, large-eyed needle in a pin cushion, small spool of thread, pins, assorted pieces of material cut into shapes for doll clothes, articles for decorating clothes such as fur, ribbon, cotton or yarn.

*Projects for Scout Troops:*

1. Cut out interesting pictures from magazines and organize them in large manila envelopes so that children can make their own scrapbooks.

2. Make simple musical instruments (bells on elastic to put on the wrist, drums, bottles of different sizes placed on a rack to be half-filled with water, etc.)

3. Paint wooden spools and small wooden blocks for play (non-toxic colors, please).

4. Prepare seasonal room decorations (particularly those which can be used on windows and doors).

5. Make finger puppets (One idea is to sew faces on an old glove so that by putting on the glove, a child can have four or five different characters for dramatization on his fingers, e.g., Goldilocks and the Three Bears).

6. Make hand puppets of terry cloth or socks.

7. Make doll clothes for 12" and 18" dolls, both boy and girl clothes.

8. Set up a terrarium (with moss and plants for "woods," or desert plants).

9. Prepare leaf, rock, or insect collections with descriptions of each specimen.

## C. INFORMATION FOR PARENTS

*ABOUT YOUR CHILD IN THE HOSPITAL*

*The text of a booklet,* About Your Child in the Hospital, *used by the Cleveland Metroplitan General Hospital, follows. A simply-printed pamphlet illustrated with photographs, of a size to fit into a lady's pocketbook, this gives important information to parents whose children are about to enter the hospital. Thus informed, parents can do a great deal toward preparing the child.*

*Should your hospital wish to reprint this material as a pamphlet for such purposes, permission to do so is hereby freely granted.*

---

# *About Your Child in the Hospital*

Cleveland Metropolitan General Hospital
3395 Scranton Road      Cleveland, Ohio 44109

## When Your Child Is to Enter Our Hospital

Both you and your child may feel a lot better about coming to the hospital if you know what to expect. This little book tells the story. It will help you to explain to him some of the frightening aspects of a hospital stay and to reassure him.

Your child's doctor is _____

Pavilion _____ Division _____

## The Ward

Your child in all likelihood will be on a ward with several other children. They like to be together. Youngsters over 11 years of age, or where medical reasons require it, may be alone or with one or three other children.

We make good use of the group on the ward — the children play and live together. Those who are up eat family style. Those in bed are pulled to the center of the ward and join the eating group if they feel well enough. If your child needs to be fed, the nurse will be glad to have you feed him his prescribed diet if you can visit at meal times.

Tell him also that he will be using a bed pan or urine bottle at times, but if he is up and around he can use the toilet.

## Admission to the Wards

Children under 2-1/2 years of age will be in Hamann Pavilion, Division 7 West; those older on 7 East. If your child is believed to have a contagious disease, he will be sent to Lowman Pavilion, Division 2B. If he is a patient in Comprehensive Care he will be on 2A. On the day of admission your child's doctor will talk over with you details of his development and previous and present illnesses. He will need your written consent for the necessary investigations and treatment. The nurse, too, will want to talk with you about your youngster. She will ask you to fill out a form that will help us to understand him better and make him feel more at home.

Before you go to the hospital pack what your youngster will need: his slippers, a robe, and some toilet articles. Don't forget to bring his favorite toy or book, no matter how old it is, or a radio. Pajamas or other clothing may be suggested by the nurse later.

## Health Team

A good program of medical services for children combines the skills of doctors, nurses, dieticians, educators and other specialists such as social workers and physical or occupational therapists.

You will find many different doctors working in a hospital that is affiliated with a School of Medicine. You may meet: medical students, interns, and residents, who all work closely with the pediatrician in charge. The staff physician who took your child's medical history will talk with you and discuss the daily medical progress.

There is a doctor on call at any time of the day or night.

## Play and School

The children find many familiar activities and toys in our playrooms which are open all day long except during the rest period after lunch. You can join him in the playroom when visiting. In summer we have an outdoor play area.

If a child has to be in the hospital for more than a week, please bring his school books so we can help him with his school work and he won't fall far behind. We will gladly talk to his teacher about special needs.

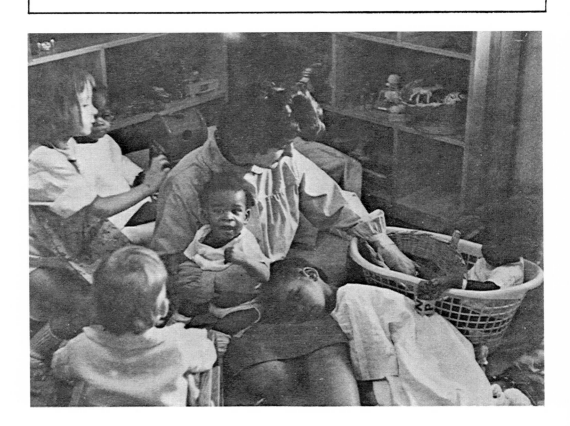

## Visiting

You, the parents, are the most important people to your child. Therefore come regularly to visit. Visiting hours are daily from 10 a.m. to 8 p.m. unless the doctor suggests a different arrangement. All visitors must be over age 16, and no more than two at a time, please!

Tell the nurse in charge when you plan to visit again so she can comfort your child if he should become sad waiting for you. Don't get upset if he cries when you leave. This is quite natural but be sure to tell him when you will be back and when his daddy can come, too. It is much less harmful for a child to cry when his parents leave than for them to stay away for fear of upsetting him. Be careful not to promise to take him home "tomorrow" unless you know about discharge plans. Tell him to ask his doctor about it.

## What to Bring when Visiting

When visiting bring things your child likes to play with and which can be kept in a small space. One gift at a time is enough. Here are a few pointers for choosing a gift: give toys that can be used more than once, like paints and paper rather than just a coloring book, - tinker toys- plastic clay - loop weaving set - a doll - paddle ball - yoyo or jacks - pencils, paper and thank-you cards - toy cowboys, Indians, etc. - puzzles - sewing kits for girls - bubble solution - model planes or boats - small windup cars. And don't forget the favorite book.

Ask the worker in the playroom for further suggestions. Remember that the hospital unfortunately cannot be responsible for the toys so don't be upset if something gets lost. Don't leave any money if you can visit often. Otherwise, leave some with the nurse in charge for an older child.

## A Few Things to Watch

FOOD: Please do not bring food, candy or chewing gum. Your child may eat it at a time when it can interfere with tests, or he might give it to another child on a special diet. After checking with the nurse you may bring ice cream or fruit to be eaten while you visit.

SAFETY MEASURES: Be careful not to leave open safety pins in the bed or on the bedside table. Always put the side rails up on the bed when you leave the bedside. Our beds are higher than your cribs or beds at home, and the hospital floors are hard.

ISOLATION: Parents can visit the child on isolation. Go first to the nurse in charge. She will instruct you in the use of gown and mask if they should be required.

## If Your Child Should Need an Operation

Make every effort to be with him before he goes to surgery. Then wait in the Waiting Room on 7 West until he returns. This will take several hours since the children go from surgery to the recovery room (which is staffed with special nurses). Be sure to be at his bedside when he returns to the Ward.

The staff will give the child as much accurate information beforehand as seems wise in a given situation. You may like to look through books that tell about an operation with your child. Ask the nurse or the worker in the playroom to give you one.

## Going Home

When your child is ready to leave the ward, the nurse or the doctor will explain any treatment which should be continued at home and tell you the date of any future visit to the outpatient clinic if this is necessary.

Be sure to stop at the nurse's desk before leaving to obtain all the necessary medications and appointment cards for your child.

If your family doctor referred you to this hospital he will also receive a letter within a few days of your child's discharge, and he is the best person to answer any further questions which arise after you have left the hospital.

DATE _____

MEDICATION _____

DIET _____

## At Home Again

On returning home your child may be unsettled for a while. He may fuss and cry if you leave him, be afraid of strangers, or be cross or difficult with other members of the family. This unexpected behaviour may be his way of expressing thoughts and fears that he is unable to put into words. A young child may not understand why he has had to go away to the hospital, or he may secretly think of it as a punishment, so be very careful never to use going to the hospital as a threat when your child is naughty.

A stay in the hospital is never an easy experience—but with time and patience your child will settle down, and be his usual self again.

THIS IS YOUR CHILD'S
I.D. PLATE IN CASE
OF LOSS.

## Some Hospital Facilities

There is a gift shop on the ground floor of Hamann Pavilion which sells the little daily necessities. A row of snack machines are at your service day and night on the ground floor of the Administration Building.

Public telephones are on each floor. If you call for information about a patient you will be connected with the Information Desk downstairs. The secretary there can connect you with the doctor if he is available or have him call you back.

Children enjoy receiving mail, so encourage relatives, friends and neighbors to send their letters addressed as follows: Child's full name - Cleveland Metropolitan General Hospital - 3395 Scranton Road - Division & Pavilion Child is in - Cleveland, Ohio 44109.

## D. "A LETTER TO BLACKIE"

*As mentioned in the chapter "Preparation for Surgery,"* this is a multigraphed booklet with line drawings. We give it to children (ages 10 to 14) who come to the hospital for an operation (except a very minor one) without preparation. Another way of using it is to have the nurse or doctor give this to a child in Clinic to take home to read once he has been told that he needs an operation. In this case we use a band around it, reading:

*Dear . . . . . . . . . . .*
*Your doctor told you that you will come to the Hospital to have an operation soon. A Letter to Blackie tells you what one youngster experienced and confided to his dog about his thoughts and fears and how all worked out well. Good luck to you, too.*

Here, too, permission is freely granted to any hospital which wishes to reprint the Letter to Blackie for use similar to that which we have found effective.

Dear Blackie:

It seems I've been in the Hospital for ages. So much waiting, waiting, waiting. What was that word the doctor said when he pressed my stomach? Wish I could remember whether we talked about that in health class at school.

It really isn't bad here. In fact I had fun painting today and I beat Joe in checkers almost every time, but it seems I just get started doing something and I'm called away.

How many doctors came to see and examine me and ask me questions? I should have counted them. There's my own doctor I see every day. He said some doctors wanted to learn about my case and that others were specialists. The specialists have been taking care of people sick like me--only I don't feel sick--for years, and they know just what to do to make me well. Well, all I can say is, then why don't they?

One doctor put a rubber band around my arm and took out some blood, and a technician stuck my finger and took out some blood. I guess I've got pints and pints and my body keeps on making more all the time, but sometimes I wonder if I'm going to have any left. My doctor said they can see how well my body

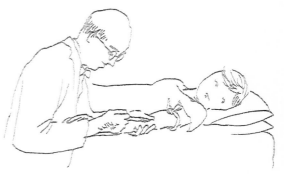

is fighting infections, whether it needs some iron or other stuff to make it work better and, I guess, a lot more things they need to know about how my blood is working.

The nurse comes around with medicine. If you're not so sick she says it's to keep out germs and if you're sick she says it's to get rid of germs. She says shots act against some kinds of germs best and pills act against other germs best. I guess that makes sense.

And then X-ray. When I see an X-ray picture, all I can see are some dark and some clear places. The big doctor holds it up and he says, "There's a clouding in the . . ."--on and on, and I'm lost, I don't know whether it's good to have a clouding or bad. But my  doctor says the pictures show whether I have any infections and if anything in me is swollen and needs attention, and so on. So the hour I spent down there to see if the picture they took came out clear was worth while.

And today my doctor told Mom and me that they're going to operate tomorrow, and he's telling me all about it. One thing I didn't expect is that if you're having a big operation in your abdomen (that's the

tummy, Blackie) the nurse gives you an enema to clean all the B.M. out.
She does that the night before the operation.

Then the doctor who gives the medicine that will help me go to sleep
came to see me too. He's called the Anesthesiologist (Blackie, what a
word to spell!) He looked to see if I had any loose teeth that might
come out during the operation and whether I still had my tonsils.
I'll tell you later, Blackie, how he's going to give me the medicine—
I'll bet it's different from anything you ever heard of. But first
I want to tell you the whole story of how the operation day is going
to start.

Tomorrow, I won't have any breakfast because food and gas don't mix,
and if you have food in your stomach, you sometimes feel sick. The
nurse said that when they are ready for me, she'll give me a shot that
will make me feel just like lying
still and taking it easy. I'll
be moved to a cart--a high bed
on wheels--and wheeled to the
operating ward to wait my turn.

Mom and Dad can see me before I go, and wait in the waiting-room until
I come back from my operation, but you, Blackie, can't come. The nurse
said that if I'm not too sleepy, I can see a lot of people in long
green robes with green masks over their faces hurrying here and there.

They wear those robes and masks to
keep any germs they might have from
getting on me. And they're green just
so the laundry knows they belong to
the operating rooms.

In the operating room, there is a
big table--rather like a cart, too. I'll be lifted onto that. The
Anesthesiologist will come and sit behind my head. About all I'll be
able to see are his eyes because
he will have a gown and mask on too.
There will be huge lights over my
head and lots of tables covered
with green towels to keep the germs
off the tools the doctor uses to do
the operation. There will be a lot of people helping
with the operation and making me comfortable.
It sounds like a pretty strange place to me,
Blackie. I wish my operation were already over.

Then do you know what the Anesthesiologist
is going to do? He's going to help me get
to sleep, either with some medicine that
runs in an I.V. into my arm (Boy, Blackie,

I'm glad it will get me to sleep
soon because I don't like needles
in my arm) or with some funny-
smelling gas that comes through
a mask over my face. (And I'll bet

you'll be surprised to hear that some masks smell like a rubber tire,
and another kind looks like my mother's
tea-strainer with a piece of gauze over it.)

He told me I'll get so sleepy I won't even
be able to keep my eyes open. But he'll be right there beside me while
the operation is going on, and the amazing thing, Blackie, is that I
won't even feel the operation at all.

The nurse said I probably wouldn't be completely awake until I got

to the Recovery Room, and that
I might wake up with an I.V.
running into my arm but that
I wouldn't feel it. In that
ward are people who have just
had operations, and they have

more nurses there to take care of you until you feel pretty good again.
The nurse will be looking at my bandage, checking my temperature and
my blood pressure to see how I'm getting along. She will help me to

turn in bed a little, because that helps me to get better faster and if my operation starts to hurt, she will give me medicine so it doesn't feel so bad. And when I'm feeling wide awake and pretty good again, I'll come back to my ward, where Mom and Dad can see me. Boy oh Boy, will that ever be good to get back!

Here comes the Nurse, Blackie, wish me luck! I'll be writing in a day or two and in a few more I'll be home again.

Hurrah!

Your Pal.

P.S. <u>Some</u> <u>days</u> <u>later</u>: Guess what, Blackie, the doctor just took out my stitches. He says I can go home tomorrow. See you soon!

*From the Department of Pediatrics and Contagious Diseases, Cleveland Metropolitan General Hospital. Written by Marlene Ritchie; illustrated by Kirstie Rossen.*

# E. PHYSIOLOGICAL DRAWINGS

The three drawings reproduced here are part of a set of seven which we have used in the Department of Pediatrics of the Cleveland Metropolitan General Hospital and which we have made accessible to all hospitals serving children in the Cleveland area. The full set consists of:

Outline of a boy's body (reproduced here).
Outline of a girl's body.
Boy's body with G.I. tract shown.
Girl's body with G.I. tract shown (reproduced here).
Boy's body with cardio-vascular and urinary system shown.
Girl's body with cardio-vascular and urinary system shown (reproduced here).
Outline drawing of doctor and child patient, and magnified line drawing of the oral cavity.

The drawings are on standard letter-size (8½ x 11 inches) paper. The cardio-vascular system is drawn in red and blue (shown here in white and gray), all other drawings are black on white.

As discussed in the chapter "Preparation for Surgery," we have found these drawings helpful. They should be considered expendable supplies. The outline of a child's body in particular gives him a framework in which he can draw his own ideas or have the adult draw in his explanation.

The colored picture of the cardio-vascular system may be used for a variety of explanations: e.g., the drawing of blood from a vein and how this helps to understand ailments of the lungs and kidneys; cardiac catheterization; glomerulonephritis; cardiac conditions causing inadequate aeration of the blood, edema, etc.

We consider these drawings still as in the experimental stage, and we hope that they will be further improved.

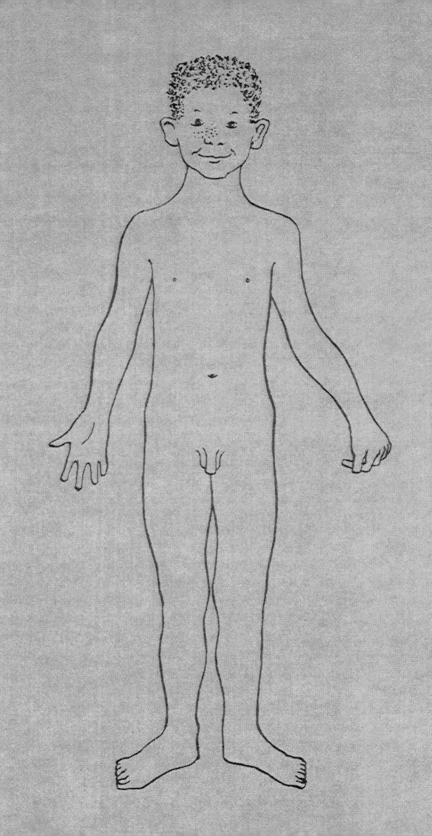

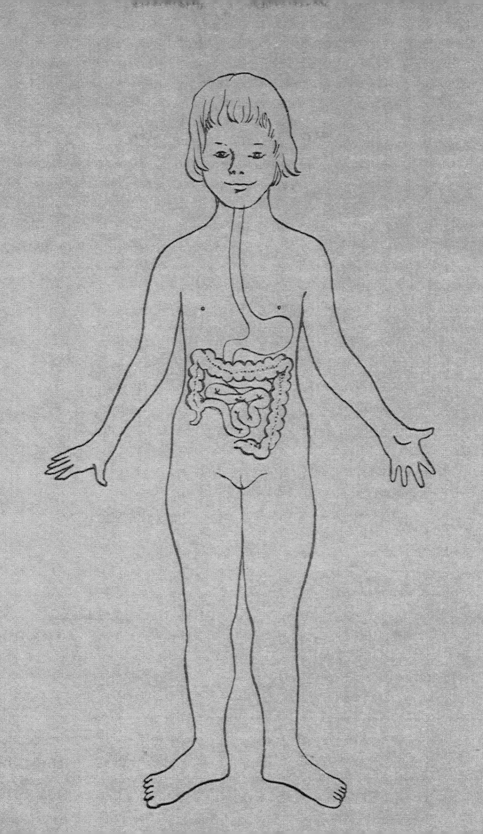

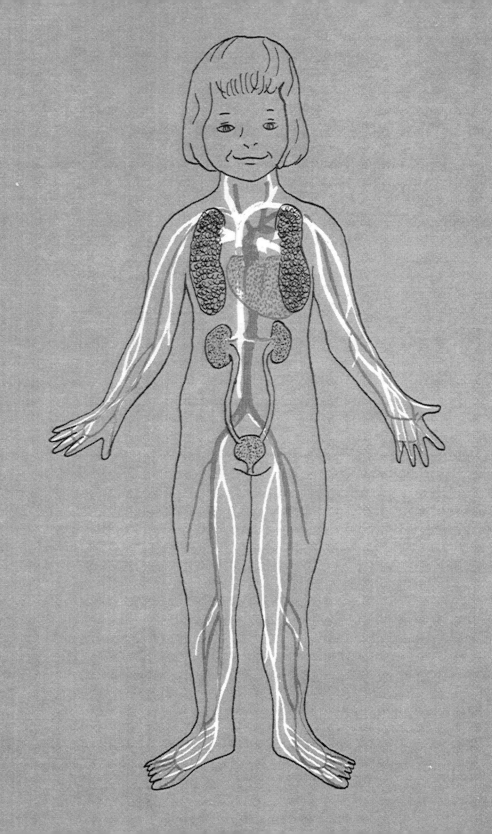

# *Bibliography*

Some Background Reading for the Professional Worker

Beers, N., "Helping the Preschool Blind Child in the Hospital," *Hospitals* 32:32, 1958.

Bergmann, T. in collaboration with A. Freud, *Children in the Hospital*. New York: International Universities Press, 1965.

Blake, F. G., *The Child, His Parents and the Nurse*. Philadelphia: Lippincott, 1954.

Blumgart, E. and Korsch, B., "Pediatric Recreation: An Approach to Meeting the Emotional Needs of Hospitalized Children," *Pediatrics*, 34: 133:36, 1964.

Bowlby, J., "A Two-year-old Goes to Hospital," *Psychoanalytic Study of the Child*, 7:82, 1952.

Byers, M. L., "Hospitalized Adolescents," *Nursing Outlook*, 15:32-34, 1967.

"Care of the Child with Cancer" (Symposium), *Pediatrics*, 40:487-546, II, 1967.

Diaz, E. J., "A Death on the Ward," *Hospital Topics*, 47:83-87, 1969.

Debuskey, M., *The Chronically Ill Child and His Family*. Springfield, Ill.: C.C. Thomas, 1970.

Erickson, F. H., *Play Interviews for Four Year Old Hospitalized Children*. Monographs of Soc. for Research in Child Development, 23, 1958.

Fagin, C., *Effect of Maternal Attendance During Hospitalization on Post Hospital Behavior*. Philadelphia: F. Davis, 1966.

Flandorf, V. S., "Books to Help Children Adjust to a Hospital Situation," *The American Library Association*, Chicago, 1967.

Freud, A., "The Role of Bodily Illness in the Mental Life of Children," *Psychoanalytic Study of the Child, 7:69, 1952.*

Gallagher, J. R., *Emotional Problems of the Adolescent*. New York: Oxford University Press, 1964.

Hailer, J. et al.,*The Hospitalized Child and His Family*. Baltimore: Johns Hopkins Press, 1967.

Helfer, R. E. and Kempe, C. H., *The Battered Child*. Chicago: University of Chicago Press, 1968.

Langford, W. S., "The Child in the Pediatric Hospital," *American Journal of Orthopsychiatry*, 31:667, 1961.

Mason, E. A., "The Hospitalized Child—His Emotional Needs," *New England Journal of Medicine*, 272:406-14, 1965.

Mattsson, A. and Gross, S., "Adaptional and Defensive Behavior in Young Hemophiliacs and Their Parents,"*American Journal of Psychiatry*, 122:1349, 1966.

Plank, E. N. and Horwood, C., "Leg Amputation in a Four-Year-Old," *Psychoanalytic Study of the Child*, 16:405, 1961.

Robertson, J., *Hospitals and Children: A Parent's Eye View*. New York: International Universities Press, 1964.

Robertson, J.,*Young Children in Hospitals*. London: Tavistock Publications, 1958.

Shore, M.F. (ed), *Red is the Color of Hurting*. Bethesda, Md: N.I.M.H., 1967.

Solnit, A. J. and Green, M.,"The Pediatric Management of the Dying Child: Part II, The Child's Reaction to Fear of Dying," *Modern Perspectives in Child Development*, 217-28, New York: International Universities Press, 1963.

Tisza, V.B., Hurvitz, I., and Angoff, K., "The Use of a Playroom Program by Hospitalized Children," *Journal of the American Academy of Child Psychiatry,* 9:515, 1970.

Play and School Programs in Hospitals

Albee, C. I., "Group Work in a Children's Hospital," *Children*, 2:217, 1955.

Brooks, M., "Play for Hospitalized Children," *Young Children*, 24: 219-24, 1969.

Connor, F. P., *Education of Homebound or Hospitalized Children*. New York: Teacher's College, Columbia University, 1964.

Noble, E., *Play and the Sick Child*. London: Faber and Faber, 1967.

Smith, A. M., *Play for Convalescent Children*. New York: A. S. Barnes, 1961.

Tisza, V. B. and Angoff, K., "A Play Program for Hospitalized Children: The Role of the Playroom Teacher," *Pediatrics*, 28:11:841, 1961.

Books for Children about Hospitals

Chase, F., *A Visit to the Hospital*. New York: Wonder Books, 1958.

Rey, M. and H. A., *Curious George Goes to the Hospital*, Boston: Houghton Mifflin, 1966.

Shay, A., *What Happens When You Go to the Hospital*. Chicago: Reilley & Lee, 1969.

Sever, J. A., *Johnny Goes to the Hospital*. Boston: Houghton Mifflin, 1953 (published for Children's Hospital of Boston).

Media Medica, Pediatric Elective Hospitalization (Wonder Book No. 686), *Jimmy and Susie at the Hospital*. New York: Media Medica Inc., 1969.